Beyond the Potting Shed

Paul Rix

authors
OnLine
www.authorsonline.co.uk

An Authors OnLine Book

Text Copyright © Paul Rix 2010

Cover design by James Fitt ©

British Library Cataloguing Publication Data.
A catalogue record for this book is available from the British Library

ISBN 978-07552-0614-8

Authors OnLine Ltd
19 The Cinques
Gamlingay, Sandy
Bedfordshire SG19 3NU
England

This book is also available in e-book format, details of which are available at www.authorsonline.co.uk

CONTENTS

BEYOND THE POTTING SHED

FOREWORD

Why should anyone want to write yet another gardening book? A fair point.

What motivated me was the fact that most books out there on the subject have one thing in common, they are written to get you to spend money! As much as possible - on all manner of things - from tools to fertilizers, even a greenhouse!

Times are tough just now for many people, and likely to get tougher, so one way to save a bit of money is to 'grow your own'. For many their attempts result in failure, or end up costing more than buying the same veg at the supermarket would have done. The aim of this book is to avoid both of the above. Everyone will have their own needs and differing skills; I hope this book will help the majority to achieve a reasonable degree of success.

Attaining success in a garden cannot, in general, be bought; neither is it a form of alchemy. Mainly it is down to commonsense and to following advice from someone who actually knows what they are doing, as opposed to someone who thinks they know. Many of the tips in this book were passed on to me by 'old boys' who really did know their onions and as they have, for the most part, 'passed on' themselves, it seems only right I too should pass this knowledge on.

CHAPTER ONE

WHO'S IDEA?

"Why don't we grow our own fruit and vegetables Dear?"

I wonder how many wives have asked that question.

"Just think how lovely it would be to pop out into the garden and pick our own tomatoes or a lettuce."

I can just see men all over the country sinking deeper into their chairs, hiding behind the sport pages, already thinking of aching backs!

With ever escalating costs it does make sense to 'grow your own'. It can save money in ways other than a reduced bill at the supermarket. If you already have the obligatory neat little front garden, you can now dispense with the separate wheelie bin for the garden rubbish, which usually has to be paid for, or the regular trips to the dump. All of this stuff can go on the compost heap. Most modern houses have a neat little patch in the front and either a lawn or decking at the back. On many older estates the back gardens are simply neglected. Often such gardens are not large enough to grow sufficient crops to feed even a couple, never mind a family; even so, careful planning can make the enterprise worth while. I would not recommend renting an allotment until you have mastered the basics, but by all means take a walk to your local allotments, you will learn a lot. One point though, believe your eyes more than your ears! A quick look will soon tell you who knows what he, or she, is doing. Try to watch what the successful ones are doing. Observation will be better than any amount of books, including this one, for picking up the subtleties of what works in your area, as well as what does not!

Sit down and work out what you would like to grow - your favourites - or the vegetables you spend the most money on. Look at this list then work out what you can grow. Many factors will influence your final choice - what is the soil like? How much sun does your patch get? Trees and hedges also make a lot of difference as to what will or will not grow.

Having decided on the scale of your enterprise, the first thing to do is to totally clear the plot, right down to bare earth. You could leave any well cut grass, such as a lawn, but even this is better chipped off and added to the compost heap.

These often neglected patches can be a valuable resource in today's mad world. Self sufficiency is probably an impossible objective, but with a little thought and a bit of knowledge you could knock a significant hole in your annual grocery bill. Looking after your garden will definitely improve your fitness and home grown veg, whilst it may not always look as good as supermarket produce, will certainly taste a whole lot better, not least because it is inevitably fresher.

All this current research which states there is no evidence to prove 'organic' veg is more nutritious than the 'normally' grown crops is absolutely correct, but then I can't recall anyone seriously saying it was. The nutrient level in an 'organic' carrot is, in all probability, identical to one of the same variety grown in a field 'normally'. The more obvious difference is one looks 'perfect' and is full of chemicals, the other is full of flavour, [and probably bugs].

I am not against the use of chemicals when there is no other way. The point is, I only use them when I have to, not as a matter of course. Only use them when you have to, and then ensure you use them correctly and CAREFULLY.

An example, and this is not scare mongering, your future veg patch is full of brambles, nettles and greater bindweed. Conventional advice is to spray it with bramble and nettle killer. This advice is usually given by an 'expert' sponsored by a major chain who want to sell you the stuff and much more besides, which they try to tempt you to buy. Fine, if that is the way you want to do things. The active ingredient is usually 2.4.5T, or 2.4D - both are excellent weedkillers for tough broadleaved weeds. A by-product of the manufacture of this group of chemicals is Dioxin, the stuff which escaped from the factory in Bhopal! In fairness Britain has the strictest rules governing such things, but there is no totally safe level of Dioxin. Most people have some in their system and it has little or no effect; a tiny minority cannot tolerate it, as was proven by the careless use of 'agent orange' in Vietnam as a defoliant. All I am saying is, if you must use it, then be very, very careful. Personally I steer well clear of the stuff!

So, your patch is infested with all sorts of tough 'orrible weeds. Before you start hacking them down, carefully select the site for your compost heap. Mine is next to the fence of one of my neighbours, at a point where he has easy access on his side. This was no accident; he is more than happy to throw all his hedge trimmings, weeds, grass cuttings and the like over the fence, straight into my compost bin. This is great as I use tons of the stuff, and it saves him the expense of a wheelie bin and trips to the dump - in fact I have three neighbours who contribute to my heaps.

So you have selected the most practical site and all you need now is something to keep it tidy. I use old sheets of corrugated tin, held up by some stout posts on the outside. As you begin clearing your jungle, stack all the rubbish that will rot down in between your rows of tin, which should be about four feet apart. I close one end off with a piece of old trellis, but a piece of tin or an old cut down door works just as well, the point being you use what is available. Even wire netting tacked to posts will do the job - if that is what is handy, use it!

The reason I use tins is not only because I have some but they also have another advantage. The thing is, compost heaps need turning from time to time and, having tins which are easy to move, means I can easily access any point on my heaps, to get at the ready to use stuff whenever I need it. As my heap grows, I keep the 'open' end sloping at an angle which permits me to push my wheelbarrow straight up onto the top of the heap before tipping it out. Throughout this book there will be other little tips such as this; the reason is simple, I am fundamentally a lazy so and so. Well, why make life harder than it need be, if there is an easy way, and the result is just as good, then why make it hard?

When clearing patches of ground many people adopt what is best described as 'slash and burn' - messy and, in the longer term, less effective than a more measured approach. The way I tackle it is with a pair of shears, or a hedge cutter, carefully working backwards and forwards across the 'face' of the jungle, cutting the rubbish into small pieces as I go. The clippings are raked up regularly and consigned to the compost heap, By cutting it up small at this stage I avoid long tough bits in the compost which would make digging it out, whether to use or turn, difficult. Nothing surpasses a long straggly bit of rubbish in its ability to 'do' your back as you pull at it.

Using either shears or a hedge cutter has another advantage; anything too thick for them to cut has in effect graded your rubbish for you. The bits that won't cut are too thick for the compost heap and can be put aside to burn or, if there are a lot, hire a chipper for a few pounds - your local tool hire firm will advise you on the most suitable machine.

A couple of points to consider: anything thicker than about 2 inches in diameter is best cut up for fire wood; it may also be worthwhile picking out any material suitable for pea sticks, if you are planning on growing peas. It is also a good idea to stack these thicker pieces neatly; this will make it a lot easier when you come to chip or burn it.

You are now left with a patch of ground full of roots and maybe even a few substantial stumps. Removing these might well result in a trip to the Quacks if tackled with too much enthusiasm. There are easier ways of doing this without wrecking your back; removing each type of root has its own little 'knack'. Small brambles are easy - the trick is to get your fork in horizontally, about 2 inches below the surface, with the 'crown' of the root central over the fork. Using your legs, NOT your back, simply lift the end of the handle and the roots will tear out of the ground. Keep all these woody roots separate as you will have to burn them or take them to the dump.

With large bramble roots it is better to cut all round them with your spade first, about a foot away from the crown, then use your fork as before. This will not only save your back but lessen the chance of breaking the fork handle!

If you have larger stumps, a substantial elder bush for example, there is a technique to deal with even these stubborn things. The trick is to dig a trench around them; the bigger they are the further out the trench needs to be - as much as two feet away for a really big stump. When digging this trench ALWAYS cut any roots on the outside of the trench first, this will make cutting the roots a great deal easier. Cut it nearest the stump first, then you will have real problems with your efforts to severe offending roots as they will simply move under the spade as there is only disturbed soil to support them.

You may find it easier to cut the roots with secateurs or even pruners; really big roots are best cut with a saw, one which cuts when you pull it, such as a pruning saw, rather than a conventional wood saw.

Having dug round your troublesome stump, clearing the lateral roots, begin to dig under the stump. Always cut any root at the bottom of your hole first; you can then cut it again higher up to gain access to any others hidden behind it. If the stump is going to be too big to lift, chip it away as you dig under it. As long as you take small pieces at a time it should split fairly easily, much as a log for the fire would split. This is a job which rewards patience - brute force and ignorance will result in broken tools or a very sore back!

All that is left to do now with your roots is knock as much earth off them as you can, leave them to dry, then either burn them if you can, or take them to the dump if you are not allowed fires. Do not try to chip them as the soil and grit stuck to them will ruin the machine.

Next on the list to deal with are the nettle roots. Chop the patches into manageable chunks with your spade, then slide your fork under the mat of roots, as flat as you can, and lift, as with the small brambles. If you have missed an odd root here and there, don't get all macho with it; cut it, secateurs do a good job. Try to pull up a big nettle root and you are likely to spend more than a day or two on a board trying to get straight again, you have been warned!

Contrary to most books which say dry and burn the roots of tough weeds like nettles and bindweed, I actually put mine on the compost heap, why not? These roots are full of plant nutrients; they are after all the entire plant food store to get them through the winter, and to kick start the new growth in the spring. Any nettles which survive being chopped up then buried in a compost heap, and there may be one or two, will be killed off when you turn your heap.

Removing the odd big dock root is another way to wreck your back. Using your spade, push it in full depth, as close to the root as you can, then repeat the process on the opposite side of the root. Now get a firm grip of the dock with your left hand and push the handle back with your right hand. Wiggle the handle if you have to - make the spade do the lifting, NOT your back. It may take a little BF and I [brute force and ignorance] but should come out all right.

Rake up all the bits and pieces of rubbish lying around, dump them on the top of the compost heap, and you are ready to start digging.

If you are unfortunate and have an infestation of a wretched weed called ground elder then by all means reach for the chemicals. Look for a weedkiller containing M.C.P.A. As always, READ the instructions; however I should point out two doses at HALF the recommended strength, two weeks apart, will work better than a stronger dose. The time to spray it, or use a watering-can kept exclusively for weedkiller, is when there is good young growth. The clever bit about this type of weedkiller is, the plant absorbs it and it kills the weed from the roots upwards. Apply it at full strength and the sun comes out or the breeze picks up, then the chemical will scorch the soft leaves and will not be absorbed properly. The same applies if you use the widely sold 'glysophate' commonly called 'Roundup'; both will work well, but need time to work properly. They will kill pretty well all weeds, plants too if you get any on leaves or soft stems. Both are fairly safe once they have dried off, or come in contact with the soil, so keep kids and pets off for a couple of days and there will be no problem.

The other situation which warrants the use of weedkiller, is if you have a lot of twitch, a particularly tough and invasive creeping member of the grass family. If your soil is light and open, as mine is [lucky old me], these roots will shake out easily, however on a stiff clay soil it is the devil's own job to pick it out of the clods. If you are so unfortunate then I can forgive you reaching for the 'Roundup', just remember the pestilent weed needs to be growing well when you spray. I don't care what it says on the can, again two half strength doses will be better than one strong application; it's the same old story, patience pays off. Don't forget, this stuff will kill any plant if it gets onto green tissue. Do keep it off your plants, it breaks down in a couple of days once in contact with the soil and can then be regarded as 'safe'.

There is another way to apply weedkillers such as Roundup. You can buy a gadget called a weed wipe, or you can make one. All it needs is a piece of soft foam tied tightly to a garden cane. Dip into a diluted mixture of the weedkiller, squeeze off the excess so it doesn't drip everywhere, and dab the weed. The job's a good'un. If the offending weeds are large and growing among your plants, then there is a variation on the last trick. Stick a piece of foam to the palm of the rubber glove. Wet the foam with the diluted weedkiller, squeeze off the excess, then simply grip the weed at its base and run your gloved hand up its stem, wetting all the leaves as you go. Take care to keep the stuff off your plants and DON'T nick the 'little lady's' best washing up gloves – she will not be happy!! Equally, don't use a glove which leaks.

Always take care to avoid direct contact with any chemicals, however safe they are supposed to be, and wash your hands before eating or smoking if you have been using them. I know it sounds obvious but it is surprising how many people forget the basics - these things are, after all, poisons. I don't like using them but on occasions they do offer the best solution if used correctly.

One other little point, if you use a weedkiller, keep it off your boots! It is amazing how many lawns have a row of footprints across them marked out with patches of dead grass.

CHAPTER TWO

TOOLS

Before we go any further, I think it would be a good idea to say a bit about which tools to buy; it is possible to spend a fortune on all manner of 'labour saving' gizmos.

I suppose the first thing to deal with is getting the right wheelbarrow. For anything greater than the 'pocket handkerchief' of the modern estate house you will need a decent wheelbarrow. If you have a reasonable size garden or allotment do not make the mistake of getting one of those tiny galvanised abominations with a narrow solid tyre. They will sink into soft soil and become next to impossible to push; try to pull them and this usually results in a hand grip coming off! They are also so short and low, all the weight goes on your back if you stoop; stand up and you tip most of the contents out onto the wheel. They also tend to be extremely flimsy; sooner or later you will put something in them which will cause a radical redesign in the angles of the handles or the wheel!

The ideal type is a contractors' barrow; these are available from builders' merchants and have a wide pneumatic tyre; they also have strong handles. Select a barrow which has stoppers in the end of the handles. This is important as they will prevent water getting into the framework and causing hidden rust! Such a barrow will fit easily in most family cars, with the back seats down, so don't take the kids when you go to buy one! The other thing to remember is to put it in upside down, then, if you stop a little on the abrupt side, the barrow won't join you in the front of the car. When not in use always leave your barrow on its side or, better still, tipped up against a wall. Never leave it the right way up. If it rains then it will become a water tank on wheels and will rust! Ideally keep it in your shed if you have one. This type of wheelbarrow has another very important use - with the handles on the ground and the wheel in the air, it makes quite a comfortable seat - ideal when having a cuppa, or a crafty fag! Why make the job hard?

I mentioned secateurs earlier. More so than with many tools, it pays to get a 'branded' pair as the 'patented' pretty ones with plastic handles tend to break if left in the sun after a while. Get a good solid pair. I prefer the type with an 'anvil' and the top blade comes down in the centre of the anvil, rather than the type with the blade slicing down beside the stronger bottom blade. Always get one with a heavy top [cutting] blade with a rounded tip, these will last much longer than a light, pointed blade and are more resistant to abuse; even so, avoid twisting them; this is what wrecks most secateurs, so cut straight!

Now, while it may be a matter of personal choice as to which type of secateurs you use, there is no such easy option when it comes to choosing what is arguably the most important of your tools, your spade. There is no substitute for a good spade; the extra couple of pounds spent buying a stainless steel spade will be repaid many times over. Not only will it outlast any other, it will also make the job of digging a great deal easier, resulting in a lot less backache!

Being 'old' I will use 'old' measurements throughout this book, not out of spite against political correctness but for the simple reason younger people are less likely to make a mistake converting the numbers than I am, at least I hope this proves to be the case.

My spade is about as near to being 'perfect' for my needs as anyone is likely to get. I am of average size, or maybe a little under. The blade of the spade measures 71/2 inches wide and 11 inches long; this is a pretty standard size. Many such spades are fitted with a plastic covered handle; this is fine to a point. Such handles are usually attached by a metal cone made of mild steel and pinned in place, hidden inside the hollow shaft of the spade, gently rusting! The solution is easy - buy a spare wooden handle with a 'D' shaped grip at the local market, then, when the original breaks, as it will sooner rather than later, you will have the new one to fit. It is quite easy; you don't need to be a DIY expert. One thing though, take your time and make certain the new one is a perfect fit; it will need a bit of shaving down to achieve a snug fit.

As to the length of a spade, this is down to what you feel comfortable with. The overall length of my spade, from the cutting edge to the top of the handle is between 42 and 43 inches, just a smidgen more than three and a half feet. Maybe it would be more relevant to measure from the top of the blade, so as to achieve the same level of comfort with a fork, as the tines are usually longer than the blade of a spade. I am about 5ft 9ins and a little bit tall - this should give you a bit of an idea what will be ideal for you. A big mistake and a foolproof way of getting backache is to get a handle which is a couple of inches too LONG. Logic says this would mean you are not bending as much and this should be good; in fact you are better off bending properly - bending a little bit is certain to get you right where it hurts! So before you start in earnest make certain your spade feels right for you.

One other little tip, if your soil is full of tough roots, remember we are talking about digging it for the first time, then it might be worth sharpening your spade a little. Some, though not all, stainless steel spades are quite thick and relatively blunt and will be difficult to push through a mat of roots. When, or if, you sharpen your spade, always sharpen the face of the blade, never the back; also, this is a spade, so don't try to get it too sharp; overdo it and every stone you hit will blunt it again. To keep your spade in tip top nick, always clean it when you stop for the day. Ideally finish off by wiping the blade over with an oily rag or paint brush dipped in oil; this will really make a difference over a period of time.

As to the ideal fork - as I mentioned earlier, the tines tend to be longer than the blade of a spade so, as a guide, get the handles level and if the top of the tines line up with the top of the blade of your spade, then it should be about right.

As with spades, forks come in all sorts of shapes and sizes. For most tasks in most gardens the best type will have flat, straight, pointed tines about a foot long. These are usually fitted with the same type of handles as the stainless steel spades and encounter the same problems eventually. The remedy is the same, buy a wooden one.

Even with the weak handle joints, it is still worth getting the stainless steel set of spade and fork as they really will prove their worth over the years.

The other essential tools are a rake and a hoe. Again there are all manner of different types available; we are looking for the best 'all rounder' as many are designed for specific tasks.

The most suitable rake for our purpose should be about a foot wide, straight across the top, with tines about an inch apart and no more than two inches long, and slightly curved. These rake heads are usually welded to a metal handle. Have a good look at the weld when you buy yours; any sign of a crack then don't get it! It is amazing how small a crack water can get in; water plus steel equals rust!

The point about the rake head being flat across the top is quite important as there are many other uses for a rake than simply pulling the 'teeth' through the top soil. Used upside down, that is with the teeth pointing up, it is great for levelling things off and covering seeds. You can also use it vertically to LIGHTLY firm the soil over the top of freshly sown seeds as well as to break small clods.

The hoe is second only to the spade; some would argue it is THE most important tool in the average garden - on light soils such as I am blessed with they could be right. So it makes sense to get the right one for your needs. Do not be tempted by all the strange shapes different manufacturers have come up with - zig zag blades, push and pull types, you could fill the average garden shed with all the gizmos available.

What we are looking for is a simple 'swan neck' design, about six inches wide along the cutting edge, with the ends tapering inwards to the top which should be around five inches. This has the effect of making a point on each corner of the cutting edge, perfect for those odd tough weeds, but better still for making a seed 'drill' for sowing. Over the entire blade it should be about two inches from top to the cutting edge. Of course, with all the 'health and safety' rubbish around today it is impossible to buy a sharp hoe, so you will need a file. As with the spade it is important to sharpen the correct side of the blade. In this case it is the side away from you, so the flat edge is towards you.

Again I am lucky, I have the perfect hoe. My dad made it for me forty years ago! And it is as good today as the day he made it. He took a worn out mild steel hoe, cut it down so the blade was only about an inch deep and four inches wide. The new blade was, and still is, six inches along the cutting edge and five inches across the top, leaving the ideal 'point' on either end of the cutting edge - the blade is still two inches deep. The really clever bit was what he made it, and others like it, out of. Dad was a 'handy man' of the highest order; when one of his saws got to the point he could no longer sharpen it, he cut the super hard steel into hoe blades and riveted them to worn out hoes.

The result was a light, slightly flexible, sharp, near wear-proof hoe, which I use to this day. Thanks Dad.

A little aside - it should be remembered 40 years or more ago things were vastly different on farms, and weed control in crops such as sugar beet was by hoeing!

So we have got our main tools - spade, fork, rake and hoe, the other handy bits and pieces, a pair of secateurs, and a trowel will cope with most jobs which need doing.

CHAPTER THREE

DIGGING

The ground is clear, the compost heap built, now the important bit - digging your plot.

It never ceases to amaze me the mess most people make of digging! It is probably the most important skill in the garden, yet it seems to be a dying art!

Digging a patch for the first time can indeed be tough going, what with all the hills and holes created by removing brambles, nettles and the like and more often than not the ground is full of roots, just to make life interesting. Digging it with a fork, so you can shake all the roots out might seem a good idea - after all the fork will go in easier than a spade. Experience however tells me this is not the case, this really is the time for a good spade to come into its own.

The first thing to do is to mark out the plot. Simply use a thick piece of string, tie one end to a garden cane, or similar strong stick. Push this in on one corner of what is to be your veg plot. Go to the other side of your plot, wind any spare string around your other stick, get your string tight and push the stick in. It is a good idea to make a small loop by simply twisting the string, just once; this will help it grip the stick and prevent the extra string turning on the stick, causing your line to go slack - a single twist is sufficient and will pull out easily when you use it again at a different length.

A couple of things to note: always start digging on the highest side of your garden, so you are facing up hill; the reason is simple, you will not have to bend so far! The other point only applies if there is a hedge; always leave a three-foot wide path beside the hedge, more if the hedge is very large. Apart from the obvious reason that this will make cutting and clearing up the trimmings much easier, it will also be a bitch to try to dig with all the roots. This may sound daft, but you would be surprised how many people try it! Why bust a gut, and probably your spade? Nothing is going to grow there anyway as the hedge will take all the nutrients and moisture out of the soil in this area. Leaving this as a path has another benefit - you will tend to keep your hedge trimmed regularly. Not only will this look smart but it adds to the vital compost supply. You can always do the last bit of tidying up by using your lawn mower to collect those annoying little trimmings which keep falling through your rake, adding yet more to the compost heap.

Back to the digging: as I said, start at the high end of your plot, using your spade cut along your line. Push it in to its full depth, this is to cut any roots from a hedge or your neighbour's shrubs on the other side of the fence. Don't do what I have seen some people do - jump on the spade with both feet! If you hit something tough, this usually has one of two outcomes, a broken spade, or occasionally a broken bone in your foot! Try tipping your spade sideways a bit, and, if you are right-handed, use your left foot to push on the top of the blade and your right hand to push the handle. If this doesn't work then wriggle it from side to side, this usually does the trick. Having cut along your 'start line', pull up one end of your line and move it through 90 degrees to mark one edge. It is easy to do a rough check to see if you have the angle right. Using your feet, measure three boot lengths along your 'start line cut' from the cane with your string tied to it, then four boot lengths along your new line. I always mark these points with a small stick and if you have got it right then it will be five boot lengths from stick to stick. My old maths teacher would be proud of me remembering Pythagoras's theory after all these years. Of course it doesn't have to be boot lengths, it could be a handy piece of stick or you could get technical and measure it! As long as the two sides are three and four, the diagonal should be five. Now you can either cut along this edge and move the line to the opposite side, or use another line. You could check to make sure the as yet undisturbed end is the same length as your first cut; if it is then you have your regular rectangle plot and life will be much easier when you start planting up with your crops.

With everything marked out, you are ready to start digging. To do it properly and effectively you need a trench and, as with most things, there is an easy way to do this. Assuming you are right-handed, start at the left-hand side of your plot. Start a few inches in from the side. If you start right in the corner your stick/cane with your line on will fall over. Work along your 'start cut' keeping it on your right-hand side; cut the opposite side of your 'spit', parallel to and a spade's width from your 'start cut' and dig out a comfortable size lump of soil. Throw this onto the patch to be dug in such a way so it breaks up; aim it at any low spots, and pick out any roots visible in your trench as you go. I always keep my wheelbarrow handy so I can throw them straight in; it saves having to pick them up twice.

When you have reached the other side, use your rake to roughly level off the soil you have thrown back and to collect the bulk of the roots. Pick up any nettle or bindweed roots when you see them. It is quite amazing how a large piece of root can simply vanish if you disturb the soil near it.

Now all is ready to start digging in earnest. Again, if you are right-handed, start at the left-hand side of your plot. Don't forget to cut the right side of your 'spit' before you put your spade in to dig. The commonest fault is to try to take too large a lump, properly known as a 'spit', don't do it! 4 to 5 inches is about right - on light, loose soil maybe 6. Digging as though it is a competition to see who can lift the biggest spade full is just plain daft! The end result inevitably looks like the aftermath of a re-enactment of the battle of the Somme! The idea is to leave a reasonably level piece of dug ground, free of the roots of the perennial weeds. Take large lumps, 'spits', and you will miss many of these roots which will then happily grow among your crops! The other thing is large lumps will take forever to rake level in order that you can sow your crops. Worse still this will mean treading around on your dug ground much more than if you had dug it properly in the first place. This will result in some of it being nearly as hard as it was before you dug it and other spots will still be soft. The effect of this will be seen in very uneven crops, not only from all the treading around but from the uneven depth of your digging.

Think about it! You have pushed your spade in to its full depth, you lean it back to pick up your massive lump, say 10 inches from the previous edge, the bottom of your spade makes an arc in the ground as it comes up. Try to imagine the shape of the surface of the undisturbed ground below. It will be a series of 'waves' - the bigger the lump you have lifted, the greater the wave. Any seed unlucky enough to be planted over the top of one of these 'crests' will only have an inch or two of dug soil in which to grow. If you don't believe me and think it is just me being a 'wimp', then try taking a single isolated spade full out of the middle of your plot. Do it carefully so it comes out cleanly in a single lump. The back, nearest you, should be clean and near vertical where the spade went in. Now look at the front! You can see my point.

Digging a piece of ground for the first time is by any definition a regular pain in the backside; it is tedious and quite frankly hard work. It has to be painstaking - small neat 'spits' picking out every piece of rubbish you can see, the more you get out now the easier things are later.

One little tip. When pulling out the roots from your trench, always pull those out from the bottom of your trench first. Pick the ones out from the top first and the roots you had seen in the bottom will have been covered up with the soil you disturbed collecting those above.

The other little skill to master when digging is - turning the spit off your spade so the turned soil ends up level; as long as you aim to keep the new surface an inch or two higher than the un-dug soil it should come out fairly level. Do this and you will find your trench gets bigger as you dig through a hole, such as where you removed a stump, or smaller if you dig over a large lump, where you buried, well, whatever! A little trick here is to throw a couple of spades full from the 'high' bit into the trench in the hollow. Easy! Don't make the mistake of trying to totally invert the soil on your spade; turn it yes, but not all the way. As long as whatever was on top is now largely in the bottom of your trench, then this is ideal. Total inversion would mean turning it a full 180 degrees - difficult to achieve. This is definitely one instance of 'nearly' being good enough.

Finally, just to reiterate, always work left to right. This will ensure a tidy finish to your work, not to mention giving your back a rest between each row. If, perchance you are left- handed then you will, in all probability, find it more natural to work with your left hand on the end of the handle and to turn the spade in the opposite direction.

It therefore follows you will find it easier working right to left.

Of course the question of what time of year these endeavours should be undertaken is a frequently asked question. Given the choice I would go for late summer/early autumn to clear a 'jungle'. Why? Well several reasons, not the least of which is the weather and the soil is more likely to be as dry as it is going to get. The advantages of this should be obvious - more pleasant to work in the sun and the dry soil will shake off the roots much easier than when it is wet. The added advantage is even a normally sticky clay will not migrate via your boots on to the patio or worse still into the house, incurring the 'little lady's' wrath.

You can always leave the bonfire until November 5th; this lessens the risk of incurring the wrath of the neighbours who could be in the path of the smoke.

CHAPTER FOUR

'CONDITIONING' YOUR SOIL

So why bother to take all this trouble; indeed why dig in the first place? Is it really worth it?

Apart from the already mentioned points of levelling and removing roots, which are fairly obvious reasons, there is another more obscure reason. You may hear old gardeners talking about 'soil conditioning'. This may sound a bit of a vague term, so allow me to explain. It is all about getting things as near to perfect as possible for your crops to grow and thrive. So exactly what is 'the perfect' soil?

It must be 'open', with plenty of air in it yet retain moisture without becoming waterlogged, so this requires it to be well drained. Something else to consider is the colour of the soil. This may seem a total irrelevance but it does however make a significant difference - a dark soil will warm up much quicker than a light coloured one, and retain this warmth much better, vital for your early seeds.

So the 'perfect' soil will be dark, open, well drained and retain moisture.

Yours has the texture of uncooked liver, has puddles two days after the last rain and is the colour of a ten-day-old British rail sandwich! Alternatively the builders have left you with a rubble strewn patch of the Sahara; after an hour of sunshine the weeds are beginning to wilt. What do you do?

The answer to both is much the same, dig it! Clean it up; get rid of the rubbish; then, at every opportunity, dig in compost! It will be months, maybe a year, before your heaps are ready to use, so what can you do in the short term to help?

Let's deal with 'the liver' first; on such 'orrible stuff you will probably have to resort to chemicals to get rid of twitch - you may not like it anymore than I do, but needs must!

You can make your life easier by staying off it when it is wet, at least when water is still lying around. Get it dug over as soon as the weather allows; this will aid the drying out process. It is important to get at least some organic matter into the soil before winter sets in. A bale of old straw from a friendly farmer will do nicely; shake it out and dig as much into every trench as you can, just ensure it is totally covered with soil.

For many of you I realise this is not possible but there are other options. Gather up leaves in the autumn and dig these in; normally I would recommend mixing them in the compost heap but your soil needs something quickly. Another option is if you had a lot of material which you chipped whilst clearing your patch - this could be dug in to help open the soil up. If you get a lot of junk mail why not shred it?. Don't use the glossy stuff though - old envelopes, even newspaper will all help. Normally I wouldn't even compost paper, I'd recycle it as there are a lot of chemicals in paper; it is all a question of priorities. Don't forget the Council will probably be running a composting scheme of some sort. It maybe worth a call; some Councils sell their compost, others are just glad to get rid of it - it is worth a phone call to find out.

There is one other alternative - if you have got your ground cleared and cleaned up in good time it may be worth considering a 'green manure' crop; these will be dealt with later in this book in some detail, so I will not dwell on them here.

On really evil heavy clays it might be worth spreading an inch or two of sharp sand on your plot - even the ashes from an open fire or Aga will help. Just don't add too much in one go; little and often over the years will eventually open it up.

As for extremely sandy soils, the sort which looks like a beach, then all the alternatives above can be applied except of course the sand and ashes.

None of the above are magical quick fixes - as far as I know there isn't such a thing. Over the years your soil, be it clay, sand, or something in between, will improve with cultivation and adding as much compost as is practical. Trying to add more than the soil can cope with will cause as many problems as it will solve. If, when you next dig your patch, much of what you dug in previously is still there other than the odd bit of stick, then clearly you have tried to add too much. What you are looking for is a nice, dark brown stain in the soil, an indication things are improving and you got it about right. Once you get a system going, you should be able to add two lots of compost every year. The longer you do this the better your soil will become, and it will at least get close enough to its optimum 'condition'. That is dark and open so it warms quickly and retains that warmth. The openness also means it drains well and the humus, the residue of all your compost, retains the moisture - which is what we set out to achieve when we started this section.

While we are on the subject of how to treat your soil, there are a couple of other useful tips which will make a difference at this stage. You've got your plot nicely dug over, reasonably level, but you are not going to be planting anything for a little while. On all but the heaviest clay it is a good idea to LIGHTLY tread it down. This is achieved by shuffling up and down, simply slide one foot past the other, keeping in contact with the ground. This helps level things up even more, lightly firms the ground and retains moisture; it also has one other effect, which is providing perfect conditions for weed seeds to germinate.

On heavy soils the only time I would firm it down is if I had done my digging in very dry conditions, and serious frosts were still weeks away. I would then dig any unplanted ground again, leaving it as open as possible to allow the frost to do its work; the only clods I would break up whilst digging would be those larger than a fist - let the weather do the rest!

Depending on exactly what weeds there are and how long it is before you begin planting, there are several ways you can deal with these. The usual way is to simply hoe it by working backwards and forwards, taking a narrow strip so you do not walk on the freshly hoed soil. The trick with this is to hoe with the blade nearly flat, disturbing the soil as little as possible, cutting the weed seedlings off just under the surface. Do this when the weeds are very small, on a sunny or breezy dry day and they will die in a matter of hours.

If, for whatever reason, the weeds are more than an inch or so high, then it is worth carefully raking the bulk of them off and adding them to the compost heap. The trick with this is to be very light with the rake, almost 'flicking' the weeds into small piles to collect; put any weight on the rake and you will collect a lot of soil as well.

The third option is to treat the weed growth as an opportunity to get yet more organic matter into your soil by treating the weeds as a green manure crop. This depends on your abilities with your spade as you need to be able to TOTALLY bury the weeds. Before you attempt this, there are a couple of things to do. Remove the perennial weeds first and any of the others with seeds already on them. If you have any doubts, hoe them off and add them to the heap! I will admit I tend to dig them in, but then I have had years of practice with a spade and can get away with it; it is of course also the 'lazy' way of doing things.

CHAPTER FIVE

PLANNING YOUR FIRST CROPS

So the ground is dug, and as ready as it is going to be. The time is right to plant your first crops, using the time scale described so far; this means starting with autumn sown crops. This is quite arbitrary, but we have to start somewhere. It is also inevitable some of the crops covered in the following pages will be of no interest to some 'would be' growers. It is impossible to grow 'some of everything' in a modern garden - it has to be left to each and every one of you to make your own choices as to what you do, or do not, grow. All I can do is pass on the basics of growing most of the commonly grown vegetables, be it to provide just fresh vegetables or to stock up the freezer. For most I suspect it will be a combination of both, if only to the extent of freezing any excess crops.

If your garden is a reasonable size, one thing to plan before you start planting is your crop rotation, as it is not a good idea to grow the same crop in the same spot year after year, with a couple of exceptions.

Below is a simple, basic crop rotation plan, using four, more or less, equal sized plots

Plot Number	1	2	3	4
1st Year	Beans, peas	Brassicas	Potatoes	Root crops
2nd Year	Brassicas	Potatoes	Root crops	Beans, peas
3rd Year	Potatoes	Root crops	Beans, peas	Brassicas
4th Year	Root crops	Beans, peas	Brassicas	Potatoes

There are very good reasons for things being in this particular sequence. Beans and peas are what are known as legumes; this family of plants have more to them than simply being good to eat. When you pull them up you will see the roots have little 'nodules' on them. This is not a pest nor a disease, these 'nodules' are home to a very valuable bacteria. These clever little devils 'fix' nitrogen from the air into a form of a salt which plants can use called nitrate - this is the stuff which makes plants grow big, green and healthy. A sign of a lack of nitrogen are yellowish, spindly, sad looking things trying to grow in your hard won veggie patch .

So we follow the peas and beans with the Brassicas - cauliflowers, cabbages and the like - which all like lots of nitrogen but not much in the way of fresh compost which we dug in in large amounts under the peas and beans which love it.

As we didn't add much, if any, compost to the cauliflowers and cabbages, we dig in as much as we can for the potatoes, although it doesn't matter too much with the earliest row.

These are followed by the 'root' vegetables - carrots, parsnips, beetroot and the like, which, by and large, do best in soil which has been heavily composted for the previous crop - as to why this should be, I have no idea. Dig in fresh compost for carrots and parsnips and you will not have too many long tapering roots. You will however have some strange twisted, multi pronged things. These will be good for a laugh and the subject of more than one dirty joke. Sure they will taste just fine, but you try peeling them!

Odds and ends, which are not included, will fit in the odd gaps - things like lettuce, leeks, onions etc. By following these basic rules, although I hesitate to use that word, you will avoid a build up of most potentially serious soil borne pests and diseases as well as getting the best from your crops.

One other vexed question we will have to deal with is where to get your seeds. Some people spend a fortune on seeds - some things you simply cannot skimp on if you want consistent results. For others, there is no reason at all why you cannot save your own. Some types I ALWAYS get from a seed company; for others 'cheapies' are quite adequate. Yet for others I rely, for the most part, on seeds I have saved myself. I will explain this as we go through the various crops as to why and what I get from where.

CHAPTER SIX

THE CROPS

One of the crops traditionally sown in autumn, also one of my favourites, is the broad bean and it is a good one to start with. They will thrive in most gardens if the soil has been well prepared with plenty of compost - a great temptation is to plant them too early. On my light soil in Norfolk I like to plant them immediately after bonfire night. In most years this proves to be ideal as we rarely get much in the way of severe weather before Christmas. Ideally we are looking for our plants to be at most 2 to 3 inches high for the worst of the weather, with no more than one leaf unfolded and another just beginning to unroll. At this stage the plants will tolerate almost anything our climate can throw at them. All the time the roots are growing away happily under the soil so as soon as things begin to warm up the plants are ready to grow away quickly. Plant them too early and they will be too big; hard frost will split the stems, heavy snow will flatten the plants. Worst of all, if it is cold and wet the plants will rock about in the wind and be attacked by a fungus disease called 'black leg' which will kill any plant it infects, and in cold, wet conditions this is likely to be most of them.

As these early sowings are going to have to tolerate the worst growing conditions then I believe it is important to use the best ed available and this means buying a packet of seed from a reliable seed company. For autumn sowings to stand any realistic chance of success there is only one type worth planting - that is 'Aquadulce'. Look for a cultivar [variety] called Claudia. This is tough, reliable and usually a heavy cropper.

Personally I would be reluctant to try an autumn sowing on heavy soils; such crops would need to be sown early to mid October to help them germinate reasonably evenly. As most clay soils will be cold and wet there is the increased risk of 'black leg'; this, coupled with the near certainty the plants will be eaten by slugs, means it is rarely worth the risk on such soils. If you have a warm corner then it might be worth a try, but the slugs may still take their toll. Not the big 'orrible slimy things of summer, but evil little grey things which live in the soil and you rarely see - these are next to impossible to kill without resorting to real poisons which kill a lot of other things as well. The only thing I know of which is effective are those products containing 'metaldihyde' - this is nasty stuff. It has its uses, but not in my garden thank you. All is not lost for those of you with heavy, slug ridden clay. The more you cultivate your soil, and the more compost you dig in, after a couple of years the grey slug population should have dropped to a tolerable level. As your soil 'opens up' and becomes less like the raw material for making bricks, these evil little things are likely to book out and move to a 'lazy neighbour's' garden where they are not constantly being disturbed.

If I am growing for the freezer then I will sow in the early spring (early March) depending on the fickle mistress, the weather. This means a slightly later crop than the autumn sown one, but seed I have saved myself will suffice for these, as they will not have to endure the harsh winter conditions. This in turn means they will grow much more quickly than the autumn sown crop, making them much less prone to disease. Also the choice of variety is less critical. To be honest I have no idea what mine are, or were. I have saved my own seed for years for my main crop for the freezer; I simply leave the strongest plants, with the biggest pods unpicked. I pick and dry the pods as soon as they begin to shrivel up; thoroughly dry the pods in the greenhouse, shell them, store the beans in a strong paper bag in a cool dry cupboard, having thrown out any 'dodgy' looking ones and they are fine.

For all the care I take in saving the best seeds, I cannot claim any great success when I have tried sowing them in autumn. I know this is because the quality seed firms dress their seeds with a fungicide, and generally take great care of their seeds. It has to be new seed every year just so I can indulge myself with those first beans of the season a couple of weeks earlier than otherwise. Add the first new potatoes of the year, a knob of butter and you realise the backache was worth it, assuming of course you like broad beans!

We are getting a bit ahead of ourselves here; we haven't even planted the things yet but it is good to hang on to such thoughts when the back starts to ache! If your soil has been dug for a few weeks and been panned down by rain, or you have been treading around on it killing weeds, then it is a good idea to disturb the top few inches before planting. This is best done with your fork. On light, sandy stuff such as mine this 'freshening up' can be achieved by simply scratching it about, effectively using your fork upside down. The same effect can be achieved using a three pronged cultivator if you have one - these are useful tools on light soils, but more on this later. Now, using your rake, level off the strip you are going to plant, avoiding walking on the soil where the seeds are going. As this will usually be along one edge of your plot you can do most of this from the path; once leveled, use your garden line to keep your rows straight. A simple piece of thick string or thin rope will suffice, attached to a couple of stout sticks. This first row should be about a foot in from the edge, literally a foot, using your boot to measure it.

The other tool you need for this is a 'dibber'. I use an old spade handle, the broken end has been trimmed to a well-rounded point, and it works perfectly. Yes, I break tools too, not often, but it happens.

Now the important bit - what we need is a row of holes, 6 to 8 inches apart and a little over 2 inches deep, but no more than 3 inches deep. Three on the lightest soils in autumn, two on clay in spring - I'm sure you are getting the idea by now.

To get all your holes near enough the same depth is quite important - the crop will then be much more even and easier to look after. The easy way to achieve this consistency is to nick a marker pen off the kids, or in my case grand kids, and put a bold ring around your dibber at the required depth. Again, there is no need to get a ruler out, the length of the top two joints of your middle finger is about right, or the length of your thumb if you prefer - both are about the same. As for nicking the pen off the kids, well why not, you'll only need it a couple of times a year. Why buy one? If yours are anything like my flock it will only get 'borrowed' by the little ones, never to be seen again. I do not recommend 'borrowing' the little lady's favourite 'bingo dabber', experience tells me this is NOT a good idea. I suppose you could always ask, but don't say I didn't warn you.

Right, back to the holes for the beans - most packets will have on them, 'sufficient for a thirty foot row' or the metric equivalent. On my patch, a big packet of beans will give me four rows, with a few left over. So I make four rows of holes with a foot between each row, that is the length of my foot, rather than the old imperial measurement. This is easily achieved by putting your heel against the stick with your line on, pulling the stick up and putting it in again against your toe, easy! I know some people who use a marker stick with all the usual distances clearly marked. Fine, as long as you remember which mark you used on the other end of your line, or where you put it last time you used it! I'll stick to my boot as a measure thank you, less likely to lose that.

Right, having got the required number of rows of empty holes, it is now a simple matter of dropping a bean in each hole. Any spares can be dropped in along the row beside the path. 'Doubling up' won't hurt if you always put them on the outside of the bed as this is where there is most light. Before you start 'doubling up' do a quick count, you may have enough for another row, but don't mess about with part rows - keep it neat and even, easier to look after.

You will always get some Smart Alec who will tell you, 'it will never grow, you've planted it upside down'. I have actually been asked by people who should have known better if it matters?!! NO, plants have a thing in them called 'geotropism' which basically means roots go down, shoots go up. In nature they would have to grow which ever way up they landed!

A couple of little tips on making your holes - when you push your dibber in, twist it as it goes in, and twist it back when you pull it out. This will help prevent loose soil falling in and making the hole one inch deep instead of two inches deep. The other thing is always make your holes along the same side of your line. If you start along the path, make your holes on the path side of your line. Move it, reach over your row of holes and repeat. If, as with my plot you will need four rows, move your line again, then working from the other side reach over your line to make the holes. This way your rows will all be the same distance apart and you will not be dragging your line over open holes - this will certainly knock soil into them.

Having dropped a bean in every hole [hopefully the right way up], before you grab your rake to cover them up remember to put a stick or some sort of marker at the end of the row[s] . At least mark the first and last rows at both ends; if you don't, how will you know where the next row will go? Now cover up the beans. You can use either side of the rake for this, but if you use the 'teeth' then use it very lightly or you could pull your beans up. Whichever side you use, finish off by using the rake vertically and gently tap the surface down with the head of the rake. Before you pull up the line, use your feet and 'shuffle' along parallel to the line but about 6 inches away from it, to give the last row of beans room to grow. This, in effect, will mark a path across your patch for access when weeding and to harvest your crop.

Keep the crop hoed; start as soon as the plants are visible, taking care not to damage the young plants with the corners of your hoe. Any weeds growing close to a plant are best pulled up. By the time the plants reach roughly 6 inches high, hoeing will become difficult. Now is the time to use your hoe to carefully draw up an inch or so of soil, creating a small ridge with the beans growing out of it. Put a stake in on each corner of your broad bean patch - a three foot long piece of wood, one inch square should suffice. If the rows are longer than about ten feet push in another about half way along either side. Run a piece of string right round the bean patch, tying it to each stake. Get the string just tight enough so that it does not sag; this should be about a foot and a half above the ground.

Do this well before the beans reach this height. As the plants reach the level of the string, simply tuck any which try to fall over back under the string. If you like you can make a large mesh 'net' by running a couple more lengths of string along the rows, then join them up with cross pieces every foot or so. Being lazy, I just 'make do' with the strings around the edges which are put up as soon as the plants are too big to hoe safely. You can't put them up sooner as it would then be even more difficult to hoe - leave it any later and you will end up doing even more damage to the plants.

Apart from removing the odd large weed which will inevitably appear as if by magic, there is only one other job to do on your beans before picking.

Broad beans attract black fly in the same way a powerful magnet will attract iron filings. These are disgusting little sap suckers! They appear as though some evil magician has put a curse on your efforts. Leave them unmolested, even for a couple of days and there will be hundreds of the evil things - few things on earth breed as fast as aphids; rabbits aren't in the same league. To make matters worse, every baby born on your beans in the first couple of weeks will be a female. These amazingly start giving birth to live young when three DAYS old, if the weather is warm. Imagine that, a grandmother to hundreds at a week old! The really bizarre thing about these promiscuous pests is the fact ants look after them as we would care for a herd of cows, to the extent an ant will attack a ladybird, whether the colourful armoured adult or the fierce mini monster larvae armed with aphid noshing jaws.

As usual there is a way to avoid this plague covering your beans with revolting, sticky, fungus-attracting honeydew. The first aphids to appear will always go for the growing points, right at the tip of the plants. The sap sucking spike these first arrivals are equipped with can only penetrate the softest tissue on the plant. We can turn this design fault of nature to our advantage by simply pinching out the growing points of the bean plants. It may seem surprising but this will actually improve the crop, not only because we have prevented an attack of the evil black fly, but because the plants will now divert their energy to swelling the pods.

A good time to remove the growing points is about the same time the first pods can be clearly seen where the first flowers had been. Simply pinch out the top inch or so of each stem. Don't worry if you seem to be removing some flower buds. This far up the stem flowers rarely produce worthwhile pods - five or six bunches of beans on each plant is the most you can reasonably expect in most seasons. I carry a plastic bucket on my arm and drop the pinched out tops into it, then, you've guessed it, onto the compost heap, black fly and all. If I have seen more than an odd one or two black fly, I will bury the tops in the heap, a sticky end for one of my least favourite creatures.

Sometimes, with the best will in the world, a weak shoot, hidden deep in the bean patch, will be missed when you pinch the tops out. You usually find it when in search of those first eagerly anticipated pods - suddenly it sticks to your arm like a black crawling version of the old 'honey trap' fly papers. Gardening is by and large a peaceful, de-stressing occupation; in this instance it is quite in order to GENTLY break off the offending, infected shoot, taking care not to disturb the little creatures happily sucking the life out of your prize broad beans. Walk very carefully to the nearest paved surface, place the poor stem on a nice flat piece of concrete, then proceed to learn the latest dance, which seems to be manic leaping up and down on the spot!

Ah, I forgot to say, do it in reach of the hose pipe - wash it off as soon as you need a rest from doing your John Cleese impression. Leave it and you could well find a cat or even a child stuck to it. You haven't got a hose, oh dear, get the scrubbing brush out before the wife gets home from shopping and wonders what the black and green stain on the patio is.

About all that is left to do with the crop now is to wait and eat your beans when they are ready. If your have grown enough to freeze some, don't forget to blanch them as quickly as possible after shelling - helps lock in the flavour if you do it quickly. I'm sure there are better books than anything I could write on the subject of freezing vegetables. Like most men, when asked to do anything in the kitchen, I just say 'yes my dear' and do as I'm told!

If you plan to save some seed for next year, leave a few plants at the end of one of the outside rows unpicked - 8 or 10 plants will produce more than enough. Remove your strings and stakes, except the stake at the end of your plants left for seed. Push one of the other stakes in next to the last plant at the other end of your short seed row, a piece of string along each side, stake to stake and the job is done.

Many books advocate digging in the old plants. On light soils such as mine, it is my opinion they are better pulled up and consigned to the compost heap. By all means chop them up a bit with a spade but onto the heap with them, roots and all. There is a good reason for this - remember the little nodules on the roots and the nitrogen mentioned earlier? Well the thing about nitrogen is it washes out of the soil very easily. A couple of heavy thunderstorms on my soil and a lot of it would have leached out and been lost.

However, if you are on the heavy clay soils there is another little trick you can use. If you have a rotary mower with a grass box, set it as high as it will go and use it to cut the tops off your old beans. Don't get too ambitious; do one row at a time then empty it straight onto the heap - it is terrific material for all the beasties in your compost heap to feed on.

Don't bother to rake up any bits on the ground - dig them in, with the roots. Take your time to dig it properly and you are ready to plant out autumn or winter brassicas, sprouts and the like.

CHAPTER SEVEN

PEAS

I love fresh garden peas; I'll happily eat them straight out of the pods. The first few to be ready never get near the kitchen.

Before we can eat these early delicacies we must first grow them! About the only difference between autumn and spring sown crops is the time of year and the varieties we plant. The preparation for both is the same. Dig in plenty of compost and at the same time remove any roots of troublesome weeds. As I support my peas using strings, I always put in my support posts before I plant the seeds. These are a couple of old 4X4 inch five foot long posts I've had for years. This is a bit of 'over kill' on my part, but I never have any trouble with my rows collapsing. There is little in the way of a more unpleasant job in the garden than trying to find a feed of peas on a collapsed row. The row has probably been blown over, usually a couple of days before the bulk of them are ready to pick and, of course, with the wind came the rain in torrents. It is a sad fact that there are just as many peas on the side of the row which is lying on the ground as there are 'sunny side up'. The summer storm which knocked them over came at the beginning of the week and you were planning on picking your crop the following weekend. It always happens like that - by the time you get to your flattened row, the leaves on the underside have gone rotten and slimy, as have many of the pods. Half of your has crop gone, for the sake of decent supports.

So, we have a post at each end, dug in nearly two spade depths, and the soil, back filled a little at a time and rammed in tight, especially around the base. This must be tight. You can stamp it down until you are blue in the face at ground level and your post will still wobble around if the bottom is loose!

We are ready to sow our autumn peas. An average packet is usually sufficient for a row roughly 20 feet long. This is, in most cases, printed on the packet. Using your trusty hoe, pull it along a line stretched between your posts. Keep the blade at right angles to your line and you should end up with a trench about 4 inches wide, as some soil will inevitably fall back in, and about an inch deep. This is perfect on most soils; now simply spread your peas as evenly as you can over the flat bottom of the trench. Remove your line after you have sown the seeds as pulling it up will inevitably knock some soil into the trench. Carefully using the back of your rake, cover the seeds. Don't rake the soil around more than you have to as you will certainly pull up some of the peas. Use your rake vertically again to GENTLY firm the soil down - job done, for now.

As far as varieties are concerned, the choice for an autumn sown crop could not be easier - there is only one - Feltham First. I know there are several others 'recommended' by different companies and various 'experts' and, in all fairness, in some situations these alternatives will be just as good, maybe even better. But on most soils, allowing for the vagaries of our weather, then good old fashioned Feltham First is as reliable as you will get.

Now the vexed question of when to plant. In one respect you have to play 'chicken' with the fickle weather gods on this one. What we don't want are plants 3 or 4 inches high to stand the winter. Ideally the plants should be an inch, maybe two inches high at the most, with a couple of good leaves on each. Frankly it is better to be a little too late than a lot too early. The best advice I can come up with is sow in mid October in the north or on heavier soils; in the south or on light, warm soils wait until the end of the month. On very heavy clay soils, simply do not bother, for all of the same reasons as with the broad beans.

As with the comments on sowing, the following applies to all peas and mange tout, which are at the end of the day simply a different type of pea. Sowing can commence in middle to late March, as ever dependant on weather and soil, later in the north or on heavy soils etc. When your peas are about a couple of inches high it is the perfect time to put in your 'pea sticks'. These are simply twigs and small branches saved when clearing the bushes; equally prunings from shrubs will do. They need to be two and a half to three feet long and reasonably stiff. Push them in, about 6 inches deep and about a foot apart, just outside the line of your seedlings. If you put a row either side, put one row opposite to the gaps in the other.

Run a string post to post along each side about two thirds of the stated height of your peas, which will be on the packet. Tie these strings together across the row about every 5 or 6 feet, now get your secateurs and tidy the sticks up, so they are all more or less the same height and are roughly straight along the edges as with a hedge.

That really is about it. You may have to add some extra strings if the crop goes mad and grows taller than it is supposed to - another reason for the posts!

On light soils the crop will benefit from having about an inch of soil drawn up to form a slight bank along either side; easy enough to do before you put your supports in, be they sticks or string. With autumn sown crops, it is a good idea to do this before winter sets in

- such supports as sticks and even the little banks offer just enough protection to make a difference.

One thing - I grew mange tout for the first time last year. Now I don't know if it was my soil or the weather, but it clearly said about 4 feet on the packet for the height of these things. I'm about five foot nine, I had to reach up to pick the top pods! I had a couple of spare eight foot long posts I was intending to use for a second row of climbing beans which I never got round to growing - lucky I had those posts!

That is about it for peas - plenty of compost, good supports, keep them weeded, and pick them before they have chance to go 'old'.

Oh yes, there is a delightful little moth, the caterpillars of which love peas as much as I do! Yes there are sprays which will kill the things; it is claimed these sprays are safe and won't kill the bees. Without the bees you won't have any peas for the 'maggots' to eat anyway, so I suppose they must work. No bees, no peas, no pea moth - makes sense I suppose.

There are also exotic pheromone traps which attract the males from considerable distances. These are sticky and trap the nookey-seeking critters into thinking the trap is a potential mate.

There is, as always, an easier way. Autumn sown crops are usually finished before the moths get about, as are crops sown in March. Sow in mid to late April and spraying will be your only hope of getting much of your crop. So if you want peas over a long period, the answer is simple. Grow two or three rows, planted in March, two and a half or three feet apart and freeze them - the same with the mange tout. As for varieties, Onward, early or otherwise, Kelvedon Wonder are reliable varieties. Trio, if you can get it, is a heavy cropper and quite tall. In truth most of the big seed firms will have their own 'special variety' and most will be good. By all means try one of these;

it could well be one is ideally suited to your patch and needs.

The other advantage of growing your peas early is the ground will be clear in time to plant out more winter brassicas, giving them a bit longer to grow bigger.

Clearing the crop is the same as for the broad beans. Pull 'em up and put them on the compost heap, unless your soil is very heavy, then, as before, cut the tops off, compost them and dig the roots in. Don't forget to remove the sticks and string first, especially if you intend using your mower to chop the tops up...... obvious? I'd have said so, but then......

The same goes for your mange tout. I can't really recommend any one variety as I don't know enough about them, only to say keep on top of the picking and freeze what you can't eat. Off a twenty foot long row we had loads, even after giving a couple of carrier bag fulls away.

CHAPTER EIGHT

SHALLOTS

These tough, yet versatile members of the onion family are often overlooked. They are an 'old fashioned' vegetable, yet highly prized by many 'tele chefs' as they have a much milder flavour than most onions. Try to buy them and they are expensive, Lord knows why, as they are one of the easiest of all vegetables to grow. It may be the recently acquired 'snob value' or, more likely, because they do not lend themselves to commercial cultivation.

There are two distinct types, each with their own use - the red ones, which are best planted in autumn, are by far the best onions for pickling - brown and crunchy, with a piece of cheese or cold meat at Christmas, unbeatable! The yellow type also pickles well, but in white vinegar, but to my taste these have other, better uses - more of this later.

As I said, these are dead easy to grow. Just rake a strip along the edge of your patch intended for 'root' crops, and push your 'bulbs' into the soft soil, leaving about one third showing. I plant my red shallots in mid October, a foot apart, which seems a trifle excessive, however there is, as always, a method in my madness. As soon as these red shallots have their little green shoots, about two, maybe three weeks after they were planted, I plant a yellow bulb in half of the gaps.

If the weather turns really foul before I plant any yellows then I will delay planting any of these until spring. This has one benefit as it will be much easier to keep the reds, which are already growing, weed free over the winter. It is surprising how many weeds will germinate during winter!

As soon as it is sensible, late February, early March, I plant the half of the yellows I had intended to plant in early November, the other half will follow in four or five weeks time.

These yellow ones will soon take on the appearance of a bunch of spring onions. As soon as they are big enough, this is exactly what we use them as - spring onions. They are superb. They can be cooked, stir fried or chopped in potato salad and are in many respects superior in flavour to the 'real thing' which at this time of year will be either imported or 'forced'. This was the reason for splitting the planting of the yellows into two - to provide a succession of young, tasty spring onions.

Don't forget to leave some of the first planting to save for next year. If you leave a couple of clumps too many, you can always get 'the boss' to pickle the extras.

The red ones meanwhile are, or should be, growing away happily; apart from keeping them weeded, there is little to do to them. Around about the end of June the tops will start to die, earlier or later dependant on the weather and where you live. This usually coincides with the last of the 'spring onions' being used.

When most of the tops have begun to wither, pull them up and leave them for a day or two, roots towards the sun. A good way to dry them off is to spread the bulbs out on a fine wire mesh, held clear of the ground - a few bricks and pieces of wood will do this. Now is the time to break up the clumps into the individual bulbs, rather than when you lift/pull them up. Break them up when you uplift them and the blackbirds will have a field day. Your neat row will look as though a flock of chickens have been scrapping it about - it will take ages to pick up all of your precious shallots. I know, I did it myself: Once!

When your crop is nice and dry, select enough to plant next time. Look for the 'perfect ones', a little bigger than average - not any of the very big samples as these will tend to go to seed. Clean off any loose soil and the loose paper like outer skin, but only that which rubs off easily. You should be left with a bulb covered with a layer of shiny, paper-like skin, still firmly attached. This applies to both red and yellow types. I keep mine in a seed tray for a bit, just to make certain they have dried off properly, before hanging them up in a net until I need them.

The remainder are thoroughly cleaned and presented to the wife to peel and pickle them. Like I'd know how to do it! Anyway, it involves the use of sharp tools in the kitchen!!

I suppose you are curious as to why I grow my yellow ones in the gaps between the reds? It's daft really, but I don't grow yellows to pickle, except any extras from my 'seed' clumps. If I grew them separately I would be left with a few clumps of yellows maturing at the end of their row and these would get in the way of the next crop. This way the couple of rows come out together, leaving enough room for something else - a row of beetroot or late carrots... whatever.

One other minor point - when you put all the old papery skins on the compost heap, cover them up! Otherwise the least little breeze will blow them all over the place! The neighbours will love fishing onion skins out of their Koi pond! That is it really as far as growing shallots is concerned.... I told you it was easy.

CHAPTER NINE

WINTER JOBS
and other options for planting in autumn

If it were my garden, freshly cleared and dug, I'd be wanting to fill it up with all manner of stuff, full of enthusiasm for my new 'labour of love'. Well there are a few bits and pieces worth planting - a row of spring cabbage, a variety called 'Green Sleeves' is about as good as you will get, planted about a foot and a half apart. It is a simple matter to work out how many you need for a row; they are usually cheap enough off a stall on the local market, that is if you like them. Personally I'm not that keen, however it is a worthwhile crop as there is little else ready at the time of year when they mature which can be planted as late as October. Remember, we are talking about plants here, not sowing seeds. These will have been sown six or even eight weeks earlier. If you do grow a row, do not be afraid to put your heel against each plant when you put it in. I don't mean stamp on it! A firm push will suffice and it will make a great difference. As with most brassicas they like firm soil. Once they have started to grow, this is another crop which will benefit from having an inch or so of soil drawn up with your hoe around the stem.

Of course, if you are confident in your digging abilities, then this maybe a chance to grow a green manure crop - a topic I will cover in more detail later.

That is about it really - once you have had a full season there will be several other crops on the go, but not in this first one.

Not that I am advocating putting your feet up for the winter! One important job is to restack your compost heap. This will make a real difference to the quality of your compost. The basics are simple - top to the bottom and the outsides to the middle. If you start your new heap a couple of feet away from the existing sloping end then you have got it about right. Keep the new exposed end and the sides straight; stack it as high as you comfortably can, at least four feet, a bit more would be better. Once you have turned and restacked your heap, leave it with a level top and sides as straight as you can; rake the old site level throwing the loose stuff onto the top of the turned heap. If the weather is mild then it might have been a good idea to have lightly cut your grass and add these clippings into the heap as you restack it. Grass clippings create a lot of heat as they rot, and a bit of heat in your heap will help the process a lot. The other thing it may be worth doing is add a little lime. I would only do this if my heap was largely made up of grass and soft hedge clippings - these both have a tendency to go mushy and therefore 'sour'. A handfull of ordinary lime on each square yard for every foot or so of height is about right. If you have a light soil, then, rather than ordinary ground limestone, it is worth getting a bag of magnesium limestone as almost all light soils are deficient in magnesium. Adding it to your compost is the easy way to cure this often far from obvious problem. To save you putting your hands in the stuff, use a four or five inch plastic flower pot, scoop up the lime from the bag and simple shake it out of the drainage holes… easy. Sort out the tins or whatever you had used and you are ready to start a new heap. If your heap is a bit on the soggy side then lay a sheet of tin on the top - it doesn't matter if the edges are not covered as these are likely to dry out anyway. It is a good idea to put something heavy on top to stop it blowing off in a gale; alternatively tie it down to the posts holding the tins up - keep an eye on the ties; tin is sharp and will chafe through string.

This is a simple if somewhat energetic exercise - some would say it is best left to immediately after Christmas. The thinking man does it just before, so he has a reason to rest his aching back… 'well it was your idea love' is the usual excuse. This in turn creates the opportunity to browse through the seed catalogues which drop through the letter box on an almost daily basis. Selecting your purchases from these is a skill all of its own and frankly, until you have got a few complete cycles of your rotation under your belt, there is little chance of getting it right.

Remember, these catalogues are designed to get you to buy what the seed companies want you to buy; these are the seeds on which they make the most profit, or a variety they have developed at not inconsiderable cost and they want a return on their investment. This is not to say the carefully laid out pages displaying the sensational 'new' variety will result in you buying rubbish, far from it. What I am saying is, until you get at least a bit of experience, learn what does best in your particular garden, stick to the old [cheaper] standard varieties. Once you have got the hang of getting consistent results, then is the time to start trying more exotic varieties. The experience gained with the basics will greatly increase your success with the more demanding types. To me this is common sense - these newer types will, in the right circumstances, if treated right, almost always give better yields than the old standards, but then they have to as they are almost always dearer.

Think of it as if you are still learning to drive; the chances are you will make a pig's ear of driving an F1. You might not crash but you won't get the full potential out of the car - the same applies to learning the skills of this job.

Talking of F1s, as you thumb through the glossy pages of pictures of the pick of the crop, you will doubtless notice the large number of varieties with F1 beside them; equally you will have observed these are also generally dearer than 'ordinary' varieties. So, what makes these mysterious F1s so special? I will attempt to explain. The great majority of things we grow in our gardens are hybrids anyway, further refined by years of careful selection of those which have shown the characteristics sought by the breeder. An example of this would be my own self-saved broad beans. I have no idea now which varieties I started off with, more than one, that's for sure. For years I kept the seeds from the biggest, strongest plants. As a result I have ended up with beans which do well in my garden. That said, it is a virtual waste of time sowing them in the autumn; sow them in the spring and I can be sure of a decent crop.

Hybrids are usually more vigorous than their parents, if a little uneven.

So how do F1s differ? I will try to explain. First of all we need something which has what is called a 'pure breeding line'; in fact we need two of these from the same sort of plant. For the purpose of this explanation of the basic principles involved, one of these parents is tall with white flowers, the other short with red flowers. If we cross pollinate these we will end up with roughly half of the resulting plants of medium height with pink flowers; the others will be half like one parent and half like the other.

To get them all medium height with pink flowers we need to ensure the pollen is all from one parent and the seeds from the other.

Not as easy as it might sound. This involves removing all the pollen producing bits from the 'mother' variety and pollinating these exclusively with pollen from the 'dad'. The result of this painstaking work is all the 'babies' will be medium height with pink flowers. Assuming of course both parents really were pure breeding lines, in other words, they would always grow 'true to type' left to their own devices. Things are, of course, a little more complicated than this but it at least gives a little insight into what is involved… it is all in the genes!

Why on earth go to all this trouble? Well blame the supermarkets! They get the blame for everything else! It is all driven by the desire for uniformity; the needs of the growers were driven by the demands of the supermarkets for uniformity, the seed companies responded with F1s.

So how does this help the cash strapped 'grow your own' family? I said at the outset of this book I would try to cover both growing for 'fresh' vegetables as well as growing for the freezer, and this is where F1s come in handy. Suppose you want a batch of cauliflowers for your freezer; it is easier if all the batch are ready at once rather than in ones and twos spread over a month - this is where the F1 scores. Where as if you are growing for 'fresh' veg then obviously the non F1, or 'ordinary' variety is the better bet. I hope all this helps clarify things, at least a little bit.

CHAPTER TEN

SOFT FRUIT

The only other things you could plant at this time of year are things such as strawberries and the various cane fruits. In fact most fruit bushes and trees are best planted in the autumn as is rhubarb. I set out to write this as though it was a sort of diary of the first year of a garden so having stressed the importance of having a plan and following it, I suppose I had better practice what I preach!

If, like me, you have got grandkids, or maybe even your own flock, you can be certain of one thing, the little darlings will love strawberries. In an ideal world these would be planted in late September, but with the changing seasons you can easily get away with planting a little later.

There is one obscure point to consider when selecting your spot to grow your strawberries. If your garden slopes and has a solid fence or wall at the bottom, no matter how sunny it may be, DO NOT plant your strawberries anywhere in the bottom half of your garden. Strawberries flower early. I am constantly asked, 'why have my strawberries got black middles to their flowers?'

When I reply 'frost'. The usual reply is, 'but there hasn't been a frost.'

The air temperature might have been 4 or 5 degrees, but with a clear sky and no wind you can get what is called a radiation frost. With few plants in your garden to stop it at this time of year, the coldest air simply runs down the slope and only stops when it reaches the wall or fence. If these extend along the sides of your garden as well then there is nowhere for this cold air to drain away. I know it sounds daft but it happens most years; in fact it is surprisingly common. This cold air only needs to be a few inches deep and every strawberry flower which happens to be open will have a black eye; this is the part which should grow into your strawberry. Tender plants might be against the wall or fence, but if they are taller they will be unaffected!

If you follow a few basic guide lines these are fairly easy to grow with a degree of success. The first and obvious thing is - prepare the soil thoroughly, ensure all the perennial weeds are removed and dig in a generous helping of the best material, compost, or farmyard manure you can get hold of. We are only talking about a three foot wide strip for a row of strawberries, so the cost of a couple of bags of horse manure from a stable or of compost from the council should not be excessive. Take into account these will be there for two, maybe three years, so you must get something into the ground before planting your relatively expensive young plants. Order enough to give you a row if you plant them a foot apart, maybe a little more, if this is what it takes to give you a full row.

The same criteria applies to growing fruit as it does to vegetables - avoid the expensive 'new' varieties until you have mastered the basics. There is one variety, head and shoulders above all the rest, when it comes to learning about growing this crop. I am rarely dogmatic about what to grow, but in this case it has to be Cambridge Favourite. It has been around for years, for as long ago as I can remember, and that is a long time. It has been the bench mark against which all other varieties are judged. For one variety to survive for so many years it has to be good; one thing is important however, and that is get your plants from a certified source. I know I am always prattling on about saving money but over the course of a year or two you will get your money back many times over.

Get the plants unwrapped as soon as you can. They are living things and need light and air. Pop them in a shallow dish or pan with a bit of water in it, taking care to place only the roots in the water. Make sure the 'crown' of the plant is clear of the surface. Do not leave them too long, three or four hours is usually long enough, at most overnight. If you can't plant them out straight away because you have to go to work for example, at least find the time to 'heel them in'. All this entails is to make a slot with your spade in an empty piece of clean ground, place your new plants in the cut, as close together as you can get them. Do this in such a way that the plants are in a single line, the crowns can almost be touching, but above the soil, and all the roots are covered. Press the soil back on to the roots with your heel, a bit of water and they will sit there happily for a week or more if need be. To make the slot there is no need to lift the soil out, simply stick your spade a little over half way into the soil and lean it back a little to leave an open slot.

When it comes to planting them in their proper place, the carefully prepared three foot wide strip, use your line to keep the row straight. This should be about eighteen inches in from the edge of your plot. Ideally this will be in the sunniest part of your garden; few things you will grow like the sun more than strawberries. Personally I prefer to plant things like this with a trowel. Simply push your trowel into the ground, tight up against the line and pull it towards you. There is no need to make a great crater, four or five inches deep is more than enough; spread the roots out a bit and firm them in, using both hands, more your finger tips and knuckles. Don't sit there patting them down with the palm of your hand. Push that soil sown, put your weight on your knuckles to get it firm, make certain the 'crown' of the plant is just, and only just, clear of the surface of the soil. Never plant strawberries too deep, it is better to err slightly the other way, to the extent a little of the root maybe visible [up to half an inch], this is particularly important on heavier soils.

One thing sticks in my mind from college days, and that is the instructors coming along behind us when we were planting strawberries and checking we had firmed them in properly. The test they used was to get hold of one leaf on a plant; if they could pull it up by that leaf, without the leaf breaking, then we hadn't firmed them in properly. With hind sight I think this was a bit over the top, but it made the point, and the college was well known for its superb strawberries... the variety? Cambridge Favourite!

As the plants begin to really get going, just after the bulk of the flowers have set fruit for the first time, long thin shoots will begin to appear; these in turn will have young plants develop at intervals along their length. Take care of these as they will produce next year's crop; keep the ground hoed and weed free. As you hoe, sweep these runners so they are parallel to the original row. If you always work the same way along the bed you should end up with a nice neat row about eighteen inches wide.

Much has been made about growing strawberries through membranes. Without a doubt these will help to keep the weeds down as well as help conserve moisture. The most often quoted reason is the claim they help to keep the fruit clean. In a field where weeds are controlled by chemicals this is undoubtedly true. However, we are talking about a garden here, and weed control is most likely by hoe and hand. It is inevitable some soil will get on the membrane and from there onto the fruit. I'm not saying don't use it, just be aware in some situations you could be solving one problem and creating another. To be honest I rarely even use straw, usually because I am too lazy to bother, and I have to say I hardly ever have any trouble. Some times a storm comes at an inconvenient time and splashes the fruit, a quick rinse under the tap solves the problem.

Much of my success is down to my good fortune in having ideal, well conditioned soil. The surface dries very quickly, yet an inch or so down retains moisture well; it is also fairly dark so it warms well and retains the warmth. At the end of the day, as with many things in your garden, you simply have to try different ways of doing things and find out what works for you.

For what it is worth, my opinion is a few soil splashes on some of the fruit is a minor problem easily rectified under the tap.

On heavier soils there are other things to consider. A membrane will provide a home for legions of slugs which will emerge at night and scoff the skin on any nearly ripe fruit they find. This in turn leads to fungal infection. Almost over night the fruit which is just beginning to ripen turns into a mushy grey ball of Botrytis. There is no real cure for this; what you can do is try to prevent it. The trick is to get plenty of air circulating through your plants. If you get this right you will prevent much of the Botrytis [grey mould] ruining a lot of your crop - at the same time you also lose most of the slugs.

It all comes back to soil conditioning. Regular hoeing, as close to the plants as possible, will keep the surface of the soil loose, assisting drainage; even work a little sharp sand into the surface if your soil is very heavy. The rest is down to looking after your plants. Don't let the crop get too thick; some of this goes back to training the runners into gaps. Keep them parallel to the original row, ideally six to eight inches away from the original line; thin the bed out a bit if you have to, by removing the weakest plants in any dense patches. While you are down there on your knees, remove any weeds and carefully pull off any dead or dying leaves. It is, I will concede, a lot of messing about, but it will keep the slugs down, as there are few places for them to hide, and it will reduce the incidence of Botrytis because the air can circulate through the plants. As with most fungal infections, Botrytis thrives best in cool, damp, stagnant conditions.

Bear in mind also, if you do use straw, delay putting it down until the last minute. The first signs of a red fruit is a good indicator the time is right. Put it down too soon and a shower of rain will soak it underneath and attract every homeless slug within a night's crawl!! The 'secret' of straw is to keep it dry and loose, then it will at least keep your families knees clean when picking your strawberries.

Early to mid September get your trowel and secateurs. Select just enough of the strongest new plants from along the edge of your bed to plant a new row. Choose the largest of the young plants, snip through the runner, either side of the chosen plant and carefully dig it out. It does not matter if most of the soil falls off as you will be planting it almost immediately; use your foot to firm down the disturbed patch of soil. Your new row should be three feet away from the centre of your original row; again the plants want to be twelve to fifteen inches apart. Simply repeat this the following year, so you now have three rows. As soon as the crop has been picked, dig up the oldest bed and consign the lot to the compost heap. Always take your new plants from the youngest row.

When you have finished messing about planting your new row and have firmed down the places you lifted the new runners from, get your lawn mower out as long as it is a rotary type with a grass box. Set it high enough so it misses the crowns of your old plants and go over your one and two year old rows. Obviously you do not go over the freshly planted rows. If you have a 'spring bok' or lawn rake, go over the beds you have cut, fairly lightly, to pick up as much rubbish as you can, including any old straw left behind. Doing this might pull out a few plants, but these will be ones with weak roots so they are no great loss, just don't go too hard.

As a final touch, sift out some compost and top dress between the rows with a layer about an inch thick, then lightly fork it in. You only need go in about three inches. For once it doesn't matter if some of the compost is left showing.

This is where you really benefit from getting good clean stock to start with, rather than some tired old plants from a friend. If you look after your strawberries you should be able to keep your own plants going like this for maybe five years before the stock weakens, usually due to some invisible virus. Often there is nothing to see; sometimes yellow or excessively crinkled leaves but as a rule it manifests its presence in the form of hard deformed fruit and generally reduced crops.

It is for this reason I would get some new plants every second year, and start another strawberry patch well away from the first. This is of course a chance to try out some of the other varieties, if things have gone well. Try one called 'Marshmellow'; the grandkids love these, so do I! But they are quicker than I am and have sharper eyes. I usually have to make do with what they have missed!

This is one of the great things with gardening. You will remember, for the rest of your life, the expression on a little one's face when they find and pick their first strawberry, all on their own. Get the little ones involved, be patient with them. If, or maybe I should say when, they run across somewhere you would rather they hadn't, after the initial GERROFF!   Don't tell them off too much; show them the results of ill treatment on something they like. One of my grandsons can be a little horror, but he loves raw carrots, so I show him what happens to his beloved rabbit food if it is trampled on.

It does work, with patience. Of course there is always bribery, even out-right blackmail. There is another type of strawberry we have not mentioned yet. This is one of my secret weapons to get the little ones on side - the alpine or trailing strawberry. I use an eighteen or twenty inch hanging basket, with a fibre liner. I don't like the polythene ones; too many things to go wrong, too hot, too wet ..... Simply plant three young 'alpine' strawberry plants in the basket. I use the compost out of an old grow-bag, but almost any decent compost will do. Look for one with a wetting agent added. This is in effect a soap which helps the water to stick to the compost. As far as watering is concerned, 'little and often' is the trick - it is important not to over water these.

If you have never tasted these 'alpines' then you will not fully understand, but to prove what an evil old granddad I am, I put the basket too high for the little ones to reach. If they are good they get picked up so they can reach - you have to see their faces!! If they are being little heathens then I eat the obvious fruit. Hey!! it works! I still have to explain the red stains to Mum, but it's me who cops it, not the kids. 'Oh Dad!! what have you been giving them now?'

Well why not, what is the point of life if you can't enjoy the fruits of your labours, literally with the little ones. Isn't this what it is really all about?

I know there is bound to be someone, somewhere, who disapproves. 'Gardens are too dangerous' so I've been told. 'There are stinging nettles in your garden and thorns.' There are indeed, it is how kids learn. So they get hold of a nettle, once! They get scratched nicking Granddad's blackberries, so what? It's life! They also beam with the pleasure of scoffing the strawberries, especially the 'alpines'.

While we are discussing enjoying the garden, have you ever
the mock shriek from a kiddie when a goldfish sucks their finge
instead of a piece of bread, or their reaction to finding their first frog!
A big male great crested newt will fuel their imaginations for weeks
with tales of 'dragons in Granddad's pond'.

We all know the potential dangers of a pond, which is why mine
has a rustic fence to stop them running into it. The kiddies can
climb through it; I can step over it, just; so what if one of them does
fall in, as long as there is an adult around. Don't panic and rush over
all concerned, as long as they haven't hurt themselves just laugh.
For sure, there is a row of paving slabs inside the fence on which to
squat to feed the fish or just watch the frogs, but the rest is soft so
they can't hurt themselves. Once they are cleaned up, a wet kiddie
is usually a happy one. No doubt some do-gooder will say I am
irresponsible concerning the little ones…tough! It is called living
and learning! Then there is always Granddad's strawberry patch!

CHAPTER ELEVEN

CANE FRUITS

This is an ideal time of year to plant such delights as raspberries, loganberries and a load of other berries. I'm not going to go into any of them in great detail as what does for one suits most.

The usual one people have a go at is the ubiquitous raspberry. Even this comes in two distinct types, early and late ones, very technical! There are actually significant differences between them, but more of this in a bit, first we have to get our canes. As with the strawberries, always get them from a reputable source. I know this is not cheap, but remember this is a crop which will be in place for several years, it therefore makes sense to have good plants.

Preparation is important and will be the same for all cane fruit; all will do better with plenty of organic material dug in, even to the extent of digging a bit extra into the bottom of each trench. Personally I wouldn't plant any of these in my first year, it is very important to get your soil cleaned up before planting what is in effect a permanent crop. Just a suggestion - grow a crop of potatoes on your chosen site, put plenty of compost in with these, then add some more after lifting the potatoes.

Which ever cane fruit you decide to grow, above all else have good strong posts at either end of each row. If you can get them, six foot long concrete fence posts are ideal. At least two feet needs to be very firmly dug into the ground. Don't forget to get the bottom of the posts very tightly rammed in; it may also be a good idea to put in an angled support at either end with a stout short post at the base of these 'props'. These will not interfere with the crops, which ever cane fruit you grow. All this engineering work may seem a bit over the top but once a wire, or maybe two wires, are stretched between the posts there will be a lot of constant pressure pulling the posts inwards, and this is before they have to support a crop.

For the raspberries a single wire will suffice. Ideally this should be about two and a half to three feet above the ground. As a rule of thumb plant the canes about a foot apart; if you have the room, then eighteen inches is probably better. As for depth - don't plant them too deeply. If you look you will see on the stems how deeply they had been in the ground before they were lifted; simply add an inch. One thing to watch however, when the nursery lift the canes they tend to tie them in bundles then 'heel' them in out in the field. When they do this, they inevitably put them in deeper, so watch out for the lower soil mark and be guided by that, not the top one.

When you have planted your canes, tie each one to the wire using ordinary garden twine. Use a figure of 8 knot; don't tie them too tightly, just enough to stop them rocking around in the breeze.

Apart from keeping the weeds away and mulching with sifted compost two or three times a year, from the growing point of view there is little else to do, whether your canes are early or late fruiting.

The difference comes in the pruning. For the earlies, also called 'floicane' varieties, as soon as they have finished fruiting, cut out these old canes and thin out the new shoots, leaving the strongest. In an ideal world the aim should be to have a new stem about every six inches to tie to the wire, this will probably take a couple of years to achieve.

Pruning the late fruiting varieties, also called 'primocane' types, is a little bit different. This is because these late varieties produce their fruit on the new canes which have just grown, rather than on the canes which had grown the previous year as with the earlies. Some people say cut these late ones right down when the crop is finished. Fair enough, but personally I cut the old fruiting stems off just above the wire, about a couple of inches above is about right. The new shoots will be growing around the base, and will still be soft, so I leave the old canes until the spring. This offers a degree of protection from the worst excesses of our weather.

With the arrival of better weather, signalled by visible growth on the young shoots, now I remove the old shoots, cut them off about an inch above the ground and thin the young ones, removing the weakest to leave evenly spaced canes to tie in when they are tall enough. Tie in the new shoots of both types as soon as they are tall enough, three or four inches above the wire is about ideal.

I always burn these old canes, the same as I do with blackberries and the like, although all the soft stuff - thinnings and the like can go on the compost. Apart from the fact these old stems will take years to rot, the main reason for burning them is a little beastie which looks like a skinny wasp but is in fact a moth . These little monsters are not as rare as many people think; they are hard to see as they have clear wings. To outsmart the poor old gardener the devious little critters lay their eggs, usually singly, in either the growing point of your cane fruit or fruit bushes, or the angle of a young leaf.

There are several different species of these things, each having their favourite plants. What the young caterpillars do is burrow their way down the centre of the stem eating the 'pith'. No, I'm not taking it; you probably won't even notice they are there, even though your crop could be reduced by 20%! Don't leave these prunings laying about as some of the moths may be ready to hatch and start the cycle again; better to burn them as soon as you have finished pruning. Do not worry about the soft parts of the plants on the compost heap. Any caterpillars will, at this time of the year, be well down the stem in the older, tougher part.

I find the best way of burning these prunings is to use an old 45 gallon oil drum; if it is a little bit rusty, so much the better. Knock some holes in it, near the bottom, and one larger hole to get your spade in to get the ashes out and stand it on a few bricks. Drop a few pieces of newspaper in and an old cardboard box; have your prunings handy and already cut into pieces which will fit easily into the drum. Light the paper, and as soon as the cardboard catches, start putting the prunings in; the aim is to get them to burn quickly, thus creating as little smoke as possible - less chance of upsetting the neighbours. Do NOT try to start your fire with petrol; all this health and safety stuff gets to you in the end! I know it is obvious to anyone with a brain, but that didn't stop one guy just along the road from here pouring half a can of fuel for his lawnmower into his oil drum full of rubbish ready to burn. He was lucky, very lucky; quite what the pilots of a couple of R.A.F. tornados coming into land at the nearby airbase made of it, I have no idea, but they must have seen it.

It is probably a good idea to wear a thick leather glove when pruning raspberries as their stems are often covered with tiny little thorns. These are very good at sticking in your skin and can be the very devil to get out. I have no idea why, but I find it easier if I only wear a glove on my left hand, using my secateurs in my right hand.

Apart from trying to pick your fruit before your flock, be they little ones or blackbirds, find them, there is little else to do.

Some people go to huge trouble and expense to build a fruit cage. I have no idea why, just as I have no idea how the local blackbird ALWAYS finds a way in. More often than not a bird after your soft fruit is after the moisture rather than the fruit itself. The answer is simple - always provide an easy drink for the birds, well away from your soft fruit, as well as a little bit in the way of food. They probably have a nest full of hungry, demanding chicks in the hedge, so a few free titbits will mean they take the easy food and leave your fruit alone.

If I have a favourite food, it has to be my wife's blackberry and apple crumble. For a few years my garden 'got away' from me, most of it is now back under control. As we, my sons and I, systematically pushed back the invading jungle, I suddenly realised we were removing our source of blackberries. We found where the old row had been; a few years of neglect had killed the plants under the wires. The brambles we were clearing were certainly vigorous and cropped well! The obvious thing to do was select a couple of young, healthy plants. I am virtually certain the 'jungle' was made up of escaped offspring of my old, original row, as I recall the variety was Himalayan Giant. If the size of the things in my garden was anything to go by, I feel confident of my identification. We didn't find any tigers, just a couple of our 'moggies'. You do have to wonder what the 'Yeti' eats, if the name of that variety is an indicator of its origin.

Suffice to say, I once more have a productive row of these delicious fruit. The arrangement of the posts is the same as for the raspberries, except for a stronger bracing post. To prevent this angled piece of wood sliding up the vertical, I simply position the top of it against the bottom wire. This crop definitely needs two wires. Pruning something as thorny as these requires a degree of care, not to mention at least one tough glove. What I try to do is tie in the long stems to the top wire; these are the ones which will fruit. As the season progresses, new, very soft shoots grow rapidly from the base. These will produce next year's crop so take care of these, they snap very easily indeed. Tie these to the bottom wire, very gently guiding them along the wire as they grow. Do this VERY carefully, you will soon find out just how easy it is to snap one off. One little tip, tie your string around near the base of the new shoot you want to tie in, leave a little bit of slack so that the stem can grow. Carefully twist the string around the new shoot in a spiral, about one turn every foot of shoot. Now tie the string to the bottom wire, not directly above the shoot, but a little way along the wire - at this time do not pull it tight. Over the next few days slide the string along the wire in the direction you want the shoot to grow; move it an inch or two every couple of days. Once the tip of the shoot is a foot or so beyond the wire, repeat the process. Tie the shoot to the wire at the point it crosses it, wind a couple of turns of string around cork screw fashion, then tie the end of the string to the wire. Do the sliding the string along trick again and with any luck your blackberries will behave.

As soon as the crop is finished, remove the old stems, cut them off an inch or two from the ground. I find it easier to cut these things out a little at a time as they tend to fight for their lives. As with other prunings from cane fruits, burn the woody prunings as soon as you have finished; of course, any soft bits can go on the compost heap - just make sure you cut them up first.. Now your top wire is clear, cut the ties on the young ones on the bottom wire and retie them to the top wire, removing any weak stems as you go. Easy! Well in theory as least! I recommend you keep a few 'elastoplast' patches handy as I rarely manage to do this job without losing at least a little blood!! and blood makes such a mess of the secateurs!

There is however an alternative - a thornless blackberry. The variety I have is called 'Loch Lomond', and to tell the truth it is the only one I know of. There may well be others but I haven't come across them. In many ways this grows more like a raspberry most years; the fruit is undeniably tasty, but I struggle to get it to grow well. I have to ask the question, 'Is it me?' It is possible this variety would do better on a heavier soil in a wetter climate than Norfolk 'enjoys'. I don't know is the answer. As I said, the fruit is a very good flavour. The only thing is my plants don't produce very much, but the grandkids love them and of course they don't end up trapped by the thorns like a fish in a net. Frankly I find this variety a bit of a pain, darned right tetchy in fact, but about one year in three I get a worthwhile crop, so as long as I have little grandkids I suppose the plants will stay. 'IS IT ME?'

If I don't give the other 'soft fruits' at least a passing mention, one thing we can be certain of is someone picking up this book will be looking for just that.

The rest of the 'cane fruits' can be dealt with the same as the raspberries and blackberries. There is nothing mystical about growing any of them, except the thornless blackberry! What has already been described above takes care of planting and pruning. Before you prune any of these, take a good look at the plant; take notice where most of the fruit was. Most, though not all, will be on shoots which grew the previous season. The rule of thumb with these is to cut out as much old wood as you can, leaving the youngest, strongest shoots to fruit next year.

Some, such as the late fruiting raspberries, will produce most of their berries next year on stems only just beginning to grow. The reason I have made a point of saying look before you snip is simple. New hybrid berries are introduced on an almost annual basis it seems. I don't grow much fruit, so if I haven't grown a crop at some time or other, I can hardly give detailed tips about it, can I? If I rely on existing text books there is the risk that what has been written before might not be the best advice and in extreme examples just plain wrong - all copying does is perpetuate the original mistake. Once you have mastered the basics it is usually possible to work out the finer points, such as what to cut out and what not to by simply looking closely at the plant. Keep in mind the fact that all of these plants need a good circulation of air around them, especially around the flowers and fruits. It is perfectly in order to remove some growth at almost any stage if you find you have been a bit ambitious [greedy] as to how many stems you have left to fruit.

There are two bush fruits which go against the general rule of fruiting on the younger shoots - these are red and white currants. Pruning these is a bit of an art form in itself as these produce most of their best fruit on older wood. The secret is to get a good structure to the bushes in the first year in particular; this may entail cutting what should have been your first fruiting branch back hard, to just four or five buds. The object of this exercise is to get three or four good strong shoots. When pruning time comes around again, cut the weakest shoot back to two buds, just 'tip' the other two or three, an inch or two is about right.

After the first two years, the 'one third' rule applies. In a nutshell this is - cut off the top third of the bush and remove the oldest one third of the branches. Ultimately you will have to judge for yourself how much to cut off the tops. As a guide, if the shoots are strong and healthy, take off just the top inch or so; on weaker growth take the full one third. This at first glance seems plain daft but strange as it may seem, the more you cut off, the more that shoot should grow.

Keep up the mulching with sifted compost and keep them well weeded, and all should be well.

Blackcurrants are different again, as far as pruning is concerned. In many respects they are similar to the early varieties of raspberries in as much as the bulk of the best fruit will be borne on the younger stems, those which grew last year. The easiest way to induce maximum growth is to cut back your plants as soon as the crop is picked. Cut out as many of the old shoots as you can and the stems which cropped this year; leave the soft new growth, these are the stems which will fruit next season. It may be worth while thinning these out, at least by removing any weak shoots. It is a good idea to burn your prunings as soon as possible, although the soft growth can go on the compost heap. Remember the clearwing moth I mentioned earlier - well the commonest one of the family is found on, or should I say 'in', the stems of blackcurrants. By the time you have picked your crop, the monsters will have chewed their way into the 'ripe' part of the stems, so it is safe enough putting the soft stuff on your heap.

Gooseberries can also be planted in the autumn As with the currants, it is a simple matter to plant them - dig plenty of organic matter in and dig all roots out. One little hint on planting any of these bush or cane fruits - watch the depth - just a little deeper than they were grown at, and spread the roots out as evenly as you can before covering them over, firming them in well with your heel.

Pruning can be a bit of a nightmare as almost every variety will have its little quirks. To go into details of each and every available type, never mind variety, is well beyond the scope of this book. If you follow a couple of simple guide lines then you should be alright. Most, though not all, gooseberries do best if you can make them grow on a stem. Think of it as a miniature tree trunk; this only needs to be about six or eight inches high, just enough to be able to get your hoe underneath to keep the weeds at bay. The other pruning 'rule' is to keep the centre of the bush open to allow plenty of air through the branches, cut out any branches going back across the centre. That is about it really for soft fruit. These bushes are quite expensive so take care of them, keep a good mulch, about three inches deep, of sieved compost around them and they will do well in most gardens.

If you have one of these bushes you particularly like, you don't have to spend a lot of money buying enough for a full row. Grow your own, it is easy, if a little slow. Some time, around mid to late October your bushes will lose their leaves. Now is the time to select a nice healthy stem of 'ripe' wood - new growth which has turned woody. You are looking for a straight piece which will be nearly a foot long when trimmed up.

Cut it off cleanly just below a bud at the bottom, a simple straight cut. Now the top needs trimming off, to remove the very soft unripe wood. Make this cut just above a bud, at a slight angle. Start at the bottom and rub off all the buds, except the top three or four. Select a sheltered damp spot out of the way of other crops, make a slit with your spade and push your cuttings into this slit, right down, so only the section with the buds remains above the soil. Tread them in very firmly with your heel and forget about them, apart from weeding and may be watering if you get a late spring drought. Come the following autumn you should have your young plants. Lift them carefully with your fork as the roots will be fragile for this first year. This technique works for most gooseberries as well as currants. If your soil is heavy and poorly drained you could add a little sharp sand along the slit before inserting your cuttings.

CHAPTER TWELVE

TOP FRUIT

It would need another book to cover this subject in detail, a thick one at that. The main variable is the pruning. Apples alone would take a thicker volume than this just to cover the different varieties, never mind all the different ways to prune them, so I will restrict myself to a few hints relevant to all top fruit, be they apples, pears, plums or any of the host of exotics now being offered to the adventurous gardener.

These are going to be growing for many years so picking the right spot is important, these things need space! The other thing is the preparation of the hole. It is no good simply digging out a crater, stuffing your tree in, covering the roots and jumping up and down on the soil to 'firm it in'. Then, when it blows over, knocking in a ruddy great stake next to the trunk means not only do you risk breaking off a branch, you will almost certainly damage the roots! The other problem with this approach is that your hole, although now full of soil, will fill with water when it rains if your soil is heavy, or if it is light, will dry out totally in a dry spell, never mind a proper drought!

These problems are not difficult to avoid. Dig out a hole at least twice as big as the spread of the roots on your tree, and at least a full spade's depth. Now use your fork to dig the bottom of your hole to the full depth of the tines; firm this down, it does not need to be hard. Half fill the hole with the best compost you have or a bag of well rotted horse manure if you can get it. Dig this in to the bottom of the hole and firm it down again. Now the sneaky bit - one thing you can say for certain is your young fruit tree will need a stake; the size of this will depend on the size of the tree you have purchased. A fairly standard fence post will usually fit the bill - the sort you hang wire on, not for panel fences. These are about four or five feet long and two to three inches in diameter and will need a decent sledge hammer to knock them in. Don't knock it straight down in the middle of your hole, you want it just off centre and at about thirty degrees from the vertical. The top of the stake should be pointing into the wind, or at least the direction you get your strongest gusts from, and just on the upwind side of the centre. This is not as complicated as it sounds. If you put the point of your post in the side of your hole about level with the top of the firmed down soil into which you dug your compost, it will be about right. If you want to make certain, stick your fork in the middle of the hole, use the handle as a substitute tree, now knock your stake in until it is within a foot of your handle. Ideally the point it crosses the handle should be almost equal to two thirds of the height of your tree once it is planted - as long as it is over half way up it will be fine.

Check to get your tree at the correct depth, about one inch deeper than it had been. Spread the roots out carefully; check again it is vertical and in the centre of the hole and within an inch of your stake. Spread an inch or so of fine soil over the roots, then grip the main stem and gently shake it up and down a couple of times, you only need to move it a couple of inches at most, this is to get soil between the roots. Add a little more soil and firm gently. Now you can fill in the rest - firm gently again using the ball of your foot, level things up and tie your pride and joy to the stake. It is quite important to use the correct method; you can of course buy a tie. I'm sure you have had a belt break! Using a one inch felt nail, these have large flat heads, nail your broken belt to the stake, about level with your tree. Put the side of your thigh against the post, then your hammering won't loosen the stake; this nail should be about one inch from the end of your old belt. Do this so as your nail is on the opposite side of your stake to your tree; bring the long end of the belt round your stake, then between the stake and the tree, round the tree, back between the tree and the stake, forming a figure of eight. Depending on whether you brought your belt back between the stake and the tree over or under the first pass, nail the long end to the stake above or below, but touching the short end. Allow for a little movement of the tree. As a guide I would suggest being able to get at least one, possibly two fingers between the stem and the tie. A little movement is a good thing, and it will also allow room for the stem to grow before you have to retie it. Add the obligatory mulch of sieved compost and the job is done. Just make sure a gap doesn't open up where the stem enters the ground and all should be well be it an apple, pear or plum.

Is it worth all this? Well yes, it is. An angled stake will give much better support than a vertical one twice the size. The figure of eight strap won't damage the bark as an ordinary piece of twine simply wrapped round both stake and stem surely will. The preparation of the hole ensures you haven't planted your expensive tree in what in effect would have been an underground pot. Putting your stake in first and planting to it eliminates the inevitable damage caused, top and bottom, by knocking it in beside your tree. And finally, the compost or horse muck ensures there is something to feed on when your tree starts to grow in the spring. Enjoy your fruit, you have earned it!.

CHAPTER THIRTEEN

ONIONS

Some of the first veg to plant in the spring time are things such as the broad beans, peas and the shallots which for whatever reason were not planted in the autumn. As these crops have already been dealt with in some detail, I will not dwell on them here, beyond saying don't be tempted to plant them in heavier soils until the middle of March, and then only if the weather is alright.

Once the crops mentioned above have been dealt with, I turn my attention to onions.

I love onions, at least the big mild ones; they are one of the most versatile crops you can grow, better yet they are fairly easy to grow, and with a little care are not normally prone to catching anything catastrophic in the way of diseases.

Should you be as keen on these eye watering bulbs as I am, then you have two main options as to how to grow them. The first option is from seed - straight forward enough - usually the first seeds to sow in spring, apart from those with the autumn option. At the end of February or the beginning of March, a few days of decent sunshine will warm the ground enough to prepare a nice fine seed bed. One thing I find which definitely helps - once I have raked over the strip I am going to plant, I get a barrow load of compost which has gone through a half inch screen or sieve, and spread it evenly over the raked ground, which I then rake again, before levelling it up with the back of my rake.

Using your line to keep straight, draw out a shallow, less than an inch deep, seed drill using the corner of your hoe and keeping the cutting edge next to the garden line. I use my hoe as it saves me bending; you can just as easily use a thin stick or piece of a garden cane. I have even seen one gardener use his index finger - well, all I can say is it must work as he always had cracking crops.

As is usually the case with these things, the 'secret' is to sow very thinly. One fairly standard packet of seed should give you about thirty feet of row. Leave a generous foot either side, maybe a little more if your soil is light and open. Before you cover the seed, push a piece of stick in at both ends of your row. This not only marks your row, so you know where it is, it also gives you something to measure from next weekend when you come to plant something else. I know it seems obvious, but you would be surprised, then again maybe you wouldn't! I have seen gardens with rows of seedlings coming up, doing just great, a foot or so apart at the path end and on top of each other at the far end. Well it does make the garden look a lot bigger, perspective is one of the main tools in the landscape designer's armoury, but this is the vegetable patch and parallel rows are the name of the game here.

I always use the back of my rake to cover these seeds as they are very shallow and easy to rake out. I also LIGHTLY firm the soil using the rake in a vertical position, gently tapping it down at right angles to the row. Using the rake across the row firms down a strip about a foot wide; this will give better moisture conservation if the weather should turn unseasonably dry.

As for varieties - well there is only one, Ailsa Craig. This has been around since Queen Victoria was on the throne. It is tough, putting up with conditions other varieties would give up the ghost and die in, and it is a good flavour, rarely turning strong. The fact it has been around so long should tell you something.

Once you have mastered growing these from seed then you can try your hand at more 'exotic' varieties, and you can always let me know how you got big onions from seed!

I freely admit, I get reasonable crops from seed, growing them like this, and the extra fine compost positively helps, but by no stretch of the imagination could my results be called good.

As I seem to be incapable of growing large onions, 4 to 5 inches across on average, from seed, I have only one option open to me - cheat!

Because of my inability to grow onions to the standard my 'O.C. Domestics' [wife] requires from seed, I resort to onion sets - small, purpose grown onions which, when planted out, produce, {hopefully} large ones. And I have to say this is usually very successful, not only in producing large juicy onions, but in keeping the little lady happy as it is, so I'm told, a lot easier to peel and slice 'one big one, rather than several small ones', like I'd know!

So, growing onions from 'sets' - As with many things, digging in a good dose of compost in advance will help things along. If you follow the way I do things, then it is quite important to keep this compost in the area to be used for the onions. As I will explain later, I usually have a row of early carrots next and these hate fresh compost.

Having dug the compost in, I then firm the onion bed down gently by doing the previously described 'shuffle' over the patch. Carefully rake it over, breaking up any clods and removing any significant stones. I have the luxury of large compost heaps, so I always have some material which once sieved resembles peat. I now add a generous layer of this stuff, normally a couple of inches deep, and 'scratch' it in using my fork. If you haven't got anything similar, it doesn't mean your onions won't grow; it simply means they might suffer a bit more if the weather gods turn nasty. Remember what I was saying about soil 'conditioning'; trying to get the soil 'just so' really pays off with onions - open and well drained yet retaining the moisture, and dark in colour to retain the warmth - this is the classic application.

Once you have got 'the hang' of growing onions, as with other crops, then by all means buy from a reputable seed catalogue. These sets will usually have been heat treated. These will, or should, have a lower instance of disease and pests such as the invisible eel worm; your crop should also be much more even and mature quicker. These advantages will however be lost if you haven't got the basics right. I still buy my sets from a market stall. It is run by a local nurseryman rather than someone who is simply a trader. This is often a good bet for a lot of your seeds and plants as he bulk buys from reputable suppliers.

I usually buy three of these standard bags. They used to hold a pound in 'old money' so I suppose these bags must contain about half a kilo, although I could be wrong. What I do is get one bag of the small, standard, sets and one of large sets, which of course have far fewer bulbs in them. If all goes well, then these will produce bigger than usual bulbs; if, as is more likely, half of them try to go to seed, them I haven't lost much, and I will still have a few big ones to 'show off' with. In truth, the standard sets produce excellent onions of a good average size. The third bag is of standard size 'reds'. I have no idea what variety these are but they grow well and eat even better. The others are usually a variety called 'Sturton' - these produce a deeper bulb than the flatter 'Ailsa Craig'.

When it comes to actually planting the 'sets', the easy way is to make a very shallow drill with the corner of your hoe; this only needs to be about half an inch deep. It is now simply a matter of pushing your sets in along this drill, ideally they should be roughly six inches apart, this is to make it easier to get your hoe between them in the early stages of growth. Push each set in about half its depth; do not cover them, leave the drill open. One thing, it is worth checking your sets on almost a daily basis as you will find they mysteriously migrate from where you planted them, at least until the roots develop. I was always told it was birds pulling them up, or cats scrapping them out. I discovered the real culprit a couple of years ago when collecting worms for fishing. As unlikely as it sounds, it is worms. The dead bit sticking up on top of an onion set is a tasty meal for your average worm. What our wriggly friend does, is suck the end of this little spike of dead leaves into its mouth, finding it cannot suck the whole thing in to digest it, it tries to drag it all back into its hole. This accounts for the fact many of your migrating onion sets are found a few inches away from where you planted them and are now roots up. Another mystery solved!

Apart from replanting any the worms have tried to make off with and keeping your crop weed free, there is little else to say in regard to growing onions. It helps if you avoid damaging the bulbs in your attempts to keep the weeds at bay. This will reduce potential pests and diseases. Onion fly, should any be around, will home in on a bulb chopped by a careless stroke of a hoe from hundreds of yards away. I must admit, I am lucky and rarely see this pest to any degree, but the eggs from a single female can play havoc on the unfortunate onion, you certainly won't be eating it!

Inevitably an odd bulb will try to go to seed. The flower bud will appear on what seems to be a thicker, stronger version of the leaves; there will be a little conical white thing on the tip. This is in fact the flower bud. As soon as you see one of these, nip it off, along with about an inch of stem, I use my thumb nail. You will still get a decent onion; leaving the stem actually helps. As it is green it acts exactly the same as a leaf in producing food for the bulb.

I usually pull my onions up when most of the tops have started to die. This is usually about a month after they fall over. By the time I pull them up only the stems of those which tried to run to seed are still standing.

Try to pull them up in dry conditions; leave them in a neat row with the roots facing the sun; after a few days it is a good idea to transfer them to a rack of some kind. Almost anything will do as long as plenty of air can get round them - old wire netting is quite good, on a frame of some kind, supported on a few bricks. It is very important to get them as dry as possible. Keep those which tried to seed separate, as these will not store well; if used first then you haven't lost anything. If you have got them dry then the old stem pulls off easily and you are left with a slightly misshapen onion.

Having got your crop well and truly dried off, you can either clean them by cutting the old leaves off, leaving an inch or so of the old dead leaves above the bulb. Carefully rub off the loose, dead, scaly bits and trim the dead roots to about half an inch before hanging them up in a net in a cool dry place.

If, like me, you are a bit of a show off, you may prefer to hang them on strings -'French onion seller style'. The only beret I have ever worn was as a soldier! Hanging your crop in this way does have its advantages and is not difficult. Clean your bulbs of loose scales and dirt, trim the roots as before, but leave the dead leaves for now. Tie a strong piece of string tightly around the neck of a good sized bulb, fold the dead leaves downwards and cut them off about a couple of inches past the string. Don't be tempted to make the string too long, onions are surprisingly heavy. You might be able to lift it but will whatever you hang it on take the weight? If you are going to hang it on a hook, now is the time to tie a non slip loop, simply fold the loose end down so you have a double length and tie a double half hitch. To so this wrap the double string round two fingers at the point it will give you the required length and pass the loop at the end of your double string between the double string and your fingers twice. Slip it off your fingers, hold the double string in one hand and pull the loop with the other, tightening the knot. Cut off the loose end an inch or so from the knot, hang it up on the hook and you are ready to start 'stringing' your onions.

The easiest way, which being a lazy individual is the way I do it is as follows: onion in my right hand, dead leaves pointing away from me laying over the onion tied to the string, these leaves are to the left of the string . I hold these in place with my left thumb, then pass the bulb round the string once, over the top of the dead leaves, slide it down so the twisted leaves sit tightly on top of the knot, keeping it tight around the string. Simply carry on until you have about eighteen inches of onions sitting tightly together on your string, you will soon get the hang of it. Getting them level takes a little practice but isn't that difficult. When your string is full, get your secateurs and trim off the loose dead leaves to tidy things up.

I keep the 'seedy' ones loose and use these first as they will not keep well. Put all the rubbish on the compost heap, remembering to bury them….. the neighbours koi pond?.... just thought I'd better remind you!

CHAPTER FOURTEEN

BASIC ROOT CROPS

I usually grow my onions on the 'root vegetable' plot. In an ideal world the rows on this plot will run north to south - this is to allow maximum sun on the plants. These rows are twenty feet long in my garden. I split my plot into beds, roughly four feet wide. To achieve this simply do 'the shuffle' about six inches away from your last row of onions; this will provide you with a temporary path to work from. It maybe worth digging this first bed again after clearing the onions. If the timing is right, it should be possible to grow some late carrots and beetroot. Both like deeply dug soil, but for once do not add any fresh compost. Rake the soil, get it fine and level, working from your temporary path; avoid standing on the freshly dug soil. Put your line in about six inches away from your 'path' and draw out a shallow drill with the corner of your hoe - by shallow I mean about half an inch. Always do this with the cutting edge of your hoe next to your line, it is easier to keep it straight, avoiding those embarrassing wiggles in your row.

As I mentioned earlier, next to my onions I plant my first row of carrots. The variety I use at this time of year, early March, is 'Early Nantes'. This will germinate at lower temperatures than most and is therefore ideal for early sowings. Sow this seed thinly - a single 'pinch' of seed between your finger and thumb should do about a foot of row. Mark your row with a piece of stick or cane before you cover it up then, using the back of your rake, resting it across your line, gently and carefully cover your seeds by drawing your rake along the row. Do not push it down, the weight of the rake is sufficient to move the soil enough to cover the seed. Don't 'fuss' over it as this increases the chance of moving the seeds, a single gentle pull will do.

Now move your line a foot further and open up a slightly deeper drill, nearer an inch deep; this is for parsnips. These are big seeds, but irritatingly slow to germinate and take a long time to get going. The weeds however are usually less obliging and grow in your carefully prepared seed bed with their usual vigour; this creates the problem of knowing where to hoe. The weeds have grown but the parsnips have yet to show themselves, as usual there is a little 'dodge' to get round this inconvenient habit.

The way I get round this is to sow little lumps of parsnip seeds roughly every six inches, three or four seeds at each station is about right. Now the 'sneaky' bit - exactly what you plant in the gaps is to some extent a matter of personal taste. The original choice used to be a few radish seeds in each gap, the variety most popular for this was 'French Breakfast'. This variety grows very quickly, even in the marginal conditions of early spring. There is no need to use just radish for this, not everyone likes them. An alternative is a pinch of rocket in each gap. If you use rocket, sow a few seeds in the middle of each gap, as this can get a bit bigger than we really want. There is no reason why you shouldn't put radish and rocket in alternate gaps - these plants are there to mark your row of parsnips. The tasty morsels you harvest from them is a bonus. Cover the row in the same way as the carrots, resting the back of the rake on the line to prevent pulling the seeds out of place. There is another little dodge you can use to get your parsnips off to an early start; this really comes into its own if we have a late spring; equally you can do this if your soil is 'lumpy' and the clods are hard to break up. I know this is going to sound like something off an old kiddies tele program, but hey, it works. Save the cardboard tubes from a couple of toilet rolls, an old newspaper and buy a cheap little bottle of clear paper gum, one of those with a red spreader on top. A couple of paperclips will come in handy and a pair of scissors - don't make the mistake I made once of 'borrowing' the boss's best dressmaking scissors, the little lady was not exactly happy about this use, now I ask!!!

The object is to make some paper tubes the same size as the cardboard tube from the toilet roll. Cut the newspaper into strips the same width as the tube is long, each strip wants to be long enough to wrap round the tube two and a half times. The easy way to measure this is to mark the tube with a pen, put the mark level with the end of the paper and roll the tube along the paper for two and a half rotations. Mark the paper then cut it to the required length, I tend to cut several layers at a time.

Using your paper clips, lightly clip your paper to the cardboard roll. Place your clips top and bottom, about half an inch from the end of your paper; using the spreader put a thin smear of paper gum as near as you can to the end of the paper, keeping it off the cardboard. Roll it carefully around the tube and glue this end down too; gently remove the clips and leave the paper in place while you repeat the process on the other tube. By the time you have completed the second one the first should have dried well enough to slide it off the tube. To give you some idea how many you will need, a twenty foot long row will need about forty [six inches apart].

An ideal container for these things is an OLD washing up bowl.

Stand all your paper tubes on end before you fill them with compost; if need be use some old drinks cups or small pots to support them if they do not fill the bowl. I find it helps to tip the bowl towards me by placing a brick under the back of the bowl when filling the tubes - this helps to prevent them falling over. Make sure the compost is moist, not ringing wet, when filling the tubes. It is now a simple matter to sow three or four parsnip seeds in each tube, water lightly and the job is done. If your bowl is deep enough you can cover it with a sheet of glass or polythene tied tightly over the bowl until the seeds germinate, remove any cover when the seedlings are about an inch high.

Plant out using a trowel when the seedlings are about two inches high; plant them, paper and all, just, and only just deep enough to cover the compost in the tube. This method will work better than pots as any disturbance to the roots will check the plants. If you get fed up making the tubes get the kiddies to do it, odds are they would do a better job anyway!

You can use these tubes as an alternative to pots for many other vegetables if you haven't got the pots - saves buying them.

For the last row of the three, once you have your line in position, 'shuffle' your path about six inches from the line, this drill is for beetroot, so the drill needs to be a little deeper than for carrots but not quite as deep as the parsnips. Again the seeds need to be thinly sown. Try to get these seeds about an inch apart; I know it is fiddly, but it is worth it. There is a reason for taking care getting the spacing - technically these are not seeds; the knobbly lumps you are planting are in fact fruits, each of which can contain anything from one to half a dozen seeds.

For these early sowings I use a variety called 'Boltardy'. Again this is an old favourite, tough as old boots from the growing point of view, but very good to eat.

As with most things in the garden, there are no hard and fast rules, the above guide is just that, a guide. If your soil is heavy then it is better to grow one of the round varieties of carrot such as 'Lisa'. If you really want to grow long rooted carrots on clay then you will have to add some sharp sand. If you do the whole four foot wide bed then this will also help the parsnips. Don't add it all in one go as this will be difficult to mix thoroughly; you may have to dig a bed three times to get enough sand mixed in well enough to do the job. This is one of the occasions when a rotavator or merrytiller can be useful to get your sand mixed properly, however, remember this will cause an element of 'panning'. At best you are going to get about eight, maybe nine inches of well mixed sand and soil, below this will be a smooth hard surface left by the blades. There is a way to break this up - use your fork, work from your 'path' on either side of your sandy bed, push your fork in to its full depth, now lean it back. You will feel it when the 'pan' breaks as the resistance will suddenly lessen; do not walk on the rotavated soil and don't try to turn it over with your fork, all you are trying to do is break the pan formed by the rotavator blades. This is important as this pan will set like concrete if left and the soil above it will be badly drained and sour, not to mention muddy after heavy rain.

If, as is often the case, the weather conspires against you with these early seeds so it is late March or early April before you can sow, you can vary the mixture of crops in these three row beds. A useful variant of the original suggestion is for those who like their parsnips. I know I've been rabbiting on about putting the first row of carrots next to the onions to help ward off carrot fly, well here is a different idea.

Parsnips need a long growing season, hence I try to get one row in as early as is reasonable. The variety I grow benefits more than most from the extra growing time, no surprise, it is an old one, 'Improved Hollow Crown'. This does have its drawbacks in as much as an early sowing will, if all goes well, give you an excellent crop of large tasty roots, however, if the weather turns dry at the wrong time then there is the risk many of these early sown parsnips will go to seed. In a perverse way, adverse weather when we would like to plant these extra early crops now helps us, as these later sowings are less prone to run to seed. If this has happened and you end up sowing your parsnips and first carrots in early April, plant rows 1 and 3 with parsnips and your first row of carrots between them.

This is a recurring theme across my 'root' vegetable bed; ignoring the temporary paths I try to alternate large, slow growing crops with smaller quick maturing types. Parsnips will still be in the ground after Christmas, or some of them will be, their tops get quite large, but before this happens the row of carrots will be long gone giving the parsnips the room they need. The same is true if you planted them earlier with a row of carrots one side and beet- root on the other, so in some ways the weather dictates the pattern of your crops. As you do more gardening, you will develop your own 'feel' as to how this applies to your garden, and every one will be different in some way. This is something which cannot be taught, but can be learnt; the best I can hope to achieve with this book is to give you the basics, along with a few of the 'tricks' which work most of the time for me.

A few further words on carrots before we move on. To keep a fairly constant supply of these popular roots I suggest sowing a row every four weeks or so. Up until mid June I stick with 'Early Nantes'. From then on, until the last sowing in late July, I use another oldish variety called 'Autumn King'. I have tried a later sowing, the second week in August, of a variety called 'Nanco' and in fairness, considering how dry the weather turned, they didn't do badly. By the looks of those which are left at the time of writing, they will have withstood the worst winter for a good many years quite well. The signs are, had it not been for a serious autumn drought, there would have been a pretty good crop. I will grow this one again; with hindsight I will probably sow it a week or two earlier next time. This is my point, you never stop learning. Even when you have had the same garden for over twenty years, you learn how to adapt what you do to your crops to allow for the vagaries of our changing climate. And one final point on what is arguably the most popular of the root vegetables - around about the end of June sow two rows of 'Autumn King' or maybe 'Nanco'. These are planted with the object of providing carrots for your winter stews and are best grown away from other carrots and left as undisturbed as possible to reduce the chances of being ruined by the dreaded carrot fly. If the soil is dry when you want to sow them, draw out your seed drills, make them an inch deep, as some soil will inevitably fall in and water these drills before you sow your seed. If it is very dry, water them twice; try to avoid knocking soil in as far as possible. Sow your seed, maybe a little thicker than the rows intended to be eaten as soon as they are big enough - note I did say a LITTLE thicker. It is important to sow these seeds as soon as the water has drained down and to carefully cover them with the back of your rake as quickly as possible. It is also worthwhile taking a little time to gently firm things down with the back of your rake, using it vertically.

Enough of carrots and parsnips, what of other root vegetables? I mentioned beetroot earlier. I freely confess this is one of my favourites. I mentioned the importance of sowing thinly because strictly speaking what you sow are fruits rather than seeds; each of these fruits may contain several viable seeds, hence the importance of careful sowing. Other than to say to maintain a steady supply,

I make four roughly equally spaced sowings from whenever I was able to get the first ones in, usually early March, through to the last one around the first week in July. With any of these root crops, the practice of watering the seed drill prior to planting if the soil is dry will pay off handsomely. I'm afraid I am not very adventurous when it comes to varieties, I stick to the tried, trusted and cheap 'Bolthardy'. The cheaper brands of this old variety can throw up some interesting results - the odd white one is not unusual, sometimes you get a real giant, just like a red sugar beet which will barely fit in a pressure cooker. I have to say these 'throwbacks' break the regular pattern of 'just so' roots; they may taste a little different but are still definitely very edible. One thing before we leave beetroot - when you pull some to cook, apart from pushing a bit of soil back into the holes, twist the leaves off, leaving at least two or three inches of the stems attached. By all means remove any dead or withered leaves completely but removing the healthy stems before cooking will result in much of the colour, and flavour, 'bleeding' out during the cooking process. Apart from a quick wash to remove any soil, take care not to break the skins as this will also induce bleeding. They skin very easily once cooked and the tops also come away easily. I still put all the skins and stems on the compost heap even though they are cooked - some books say not to, but I know of no reason why not.

CHAPTER FIFTEEN

SWEDES and other things

Another root crop which benefits from a longer growing period is the humble swede. I usually sow mine in late April - the usual one inch deep drill, ideally with a fast maturing smaller crop planted either side as these can get quite large. At least when everything goes according to plan they can get large. In a way this popular, supposedly easy to grow crop, is my Nemesis. Can I grow good Swedes? Can I heck as like!!! Oh sure there are a few good ones most years, but the majority end up on the compost heap as puny, inedible roots. Personally I think someone has put a hex on me with this crop; a stew is not a stew without a few chunks of swede in it. To cut my losses I have reverted to the cheap seed. That said, I tried a variety called 'Marian', one of 'the proper' varieties, and I have to admit there were several edible roots in the row, but by no stretch of the imagination were the results okay, never mind good. I gave my neighbour the rest of the seeds from the packet and he had a tremendous crop, so I swap parsnips for swedes, as his parsnips are like under nourished dandelion roots. Why? I haven't got the remotest idea! We both planted within days of each other, we have both been in our current houses over twenty years and both qualify for our bus passes, so neither of us are exactly beginners.

Our gardens are parallel side by side, mine is a little longer and has a bit more in the way of rubbish but that is about the only difference. We even thinned our rows out the same day. I know this because he threw his thinnings over the fence onto my compost heap!

Every year I try to grow swedes and every year everything under the sun attacks them - no matter if I sow some early and some more a month later it is always the same. Every seed it seems germinates, to the point it is painful thinning out such healthy young plants. I have on occasions resorted to watering them after thinning, just to settle those left in. They continue to grow well, and every year I get to thinking, 'this time', then without warning all I will have in the way of leaves is a network of veins and stalks, all the green bits scoffed by marauding collared doves! They never touch anything else, just my swedes, and they never touch my neighbours, yet they eat his peas. Swedes, being tough, soon recover and have a new batch of healthy leaves, just in time to feed the annual invasion of large white butterflies, well their caterpillars. I search the leaves every day for the patches of pale yellow eggs, diligently squashing them between finger and thumb, then I will have a weekend away. By the time I get home my swedes are a crawling mass of yellow, green and black evil smelling eating machines. If there are any about, these things always go for my swedes or my neighbours nasturtiums and they call them 'cabbage whites'! If by any miracle my poor plants have avoided being prematurely devoured by the wild life you can be certain of one thing, mildew. Right as rain one day, turn your back for a day and they look as though someone has sprinkled flour all over them! Yet some of them struggled on and produced an edible root. I know my soil is far from perfect for swedes, in all honesty they would do a lot better on a heavier soil, but in reality most of my failures with this crop are down to bad luck. Some of it is my own fault for being lazy. I can't be bothered to train my cat to stand guard against the doves, although it does chase butterflies!

Another thing I tried was growing them with the brassicas, as this is where they really belong, being a member of the cabbage family. This didn't help either so I will refrain from passing on 'helpful hints' on this crop, I will merely say follow the instructions on the packet, and wish you better luck than I usually have.

Turnips on the other hand do embarrassingly well! Not something I would want to eat every day, but two or three tasty young turnips with a drop of melted butter go well with a roast and Yorkshire pud - they are a nice change. These, more than any other root vegetable, are best eaten young. For me the perfect size is a little bigger than a golf ball. Because you want them to grow quickly I would suggest holding off sowing them until well into April, but if spring has come early then it has to be worth an early sowing.

The usual drill, a little under an inch deep is fine. If the soil is a bit dry, then by all means make the drill a little deeper and water it before sowing your seed. As usual sow the rows a foot apart, as I said before, literally a foot - use your boot to measure with, you won't lose that! Always sow these thinly, even then they will need a bit of careful thinning, ideally to about three inches apart. The best all round is probably a variety called 'Snowball'; you won't go far wrong with it as it seems to cope better than most with our somewhat unpredictable climate. I know some people who grate turnips raw into their salads. If this is what you like, then go for it. I'm told it tastes good, but then I don't like grated carrots either.

If you are a fan of turnips then it is essential to make regular sowings, about every three to four weeks is about right. You can sow as late as early September, which, if the weather is not too severe, will give you tasty roots right up to Christmas.

As we don't eat that many turnips I tend to sow only half a row at a time, usually the other half row is planted up with lettuce plants which I have grown in pots in my green- house. As these are usually cleared at about the same time, the first row is usually the site for the last row of this combination. I simply plant the lettuce plants where the turnips were and vice-versa. In all honesty there is not much more to say about turnips, I am certainly not going to start doing recipes.

There are all manner of other odds and ends which come under the 'root crop' banner, I suppose it is worth giving a few of these a mention in passing.

Kol-rabi is enjoying a degree of popularity at the moment. From the gardening point of view it is an excellent alternative to the mid season sowings of turnips. Treat these the same as turnips, thinning out to about three or four inches apart as soon as they are big enough. Leave a foot either side of the row, as with many other root crops. You can sow these from late April through to late June or even early July - they certainly make a tasty alternative.

Slightly more of an acquired taste is a good description for Mooli, otherwise known as winter radish. Personally I love the fresh, slightly tangy taste. If you do have a go at growing this crop, then it is worth putting in the little bit of extra effort required . These roots grow deep, so before you sow these, dig the strip you are going to use. It only needs to be two spits wide, but break up the bottom of each little trench with your fork. There is no need for the full double digging thing, just turn the top spit as normal, then stick your fork in to its full depth, lean it back until the soil 'breaks', we don't want the sub soil brought to the top. As long as you remember to take small spits then this will work just fine. If you have the space, it is worth leaving an extra few inches either side of the row as the tops can be quite substantial if they take a liking to your soil. The best time to sow this crop is middle to late June, so if your soil is on the dry side it is worth watering the seed drill before sowing. As ever, sow thinly, then thin out the seedlings to four to six inches apart as soon as they are big enough. When thinning out these, and other root crops in warm weather, it is usually worth watering the remaining plants, just to settle them back in. When they are ready to harvest, don't try pulling these up as they are deep rooted. The edible bit can easily exceed a foot in length - use your fork! Still, it's your back!

What of other bits and pieces? Celeriac is becoming increasingly popular. Unusually for a 'root crop', this is one which is best started off in the greenhouse. I sow mine in late March or, if the weather had been really horrible, I may delay until early April. As soon as the seedlings are large enough to handle safely, I transfer them to three and a half inch pots. These are usually ready to plant out in the second or third week in May. I plant these out about a foot apart, and apart from keeping the weeds at bay there is little else to do until you lift them to eat.

Fennel is another of these slightly exotic vegetables which is gaining in popularity and I must confess, one I have never grown, at least as a vegetable. I suppose the same basic growing conditions apply to the varieties bred for food as for the decorative types - they are after all the same species [Foeniculum vulgare] as the decorative types with purple foliage which I have grown. It is also the same as the common [wild] fennel which I have also grown to feed some exotic caterpillars I was rearing. Based on my experience growing these other types, it seems as though it is not too fussy; as long as it is in reasonable soil, with a bit of compost in it and doesn't get too dry or the other extreme, flooded, then it will thrive. I might try some myself next season as I have eaten braised fennel - it wasn't bad.... different yes, the sort of thing which is nice for a change.

If you do have a go at growing fennel then give it room as the feathery leaves have quite a spread. I started mine in pots in late March, then planted them out in mid May. A friend of mine grows it most years; interestingly he advises sowing it direct, then thinning the plants out to at least a foot apart; he also says leave at least eighteen inches between rows. As the only fennel I can remember eating came from him, and as I said, it was alright, it seems reasonable to assume he has got it right. He can certainly grow swedes! even if he can't grow parsnips!

The only other crop I grow in this patch in their own right are my leeks - all the multitude of other bits and pieces which appear between, before or after these principle crops come under the heading of 'catch crops'. These will be dealt with a little further on in this book.

Alright, I'll own up here and now, I do like to show off sometimes, and leeks give me the perfect opportunity. I love leeks, they are one of my favourite vegetables.

No surprise which variety I usually grow - the old, tried and trusted 'Musselburgh'. Within reason the earlier you sow these the better. I have the benefit of a greenhouse and sow around the end of January - at least, I sow some of my seed, about thirty in a five inch pot. The rest I sow in a frame outside, usually around the end of February, having kept the frame closed to help the soil warm.

Why the two sowings? Well I did say I like to 'show off'; starting some off early means they will be bigger plants when I plant them out. A word of caution - big, early plants do not automatically mean bigger leeks; get it wrong and these will 'bolt', that is run to seed, not what we want at all. For my row of big leeks I dig out a trench, the full depth of my spade; this is then half filled with the best sifted compost I have. I dig this into the bottom of the trench using my fork, taking care to mix it in well. I now add some more compost, almost, but not quite filling the trench, and I dig it again. The remaining soil is left in two neat rows along either side of the trench, as it will be needed later.

The perfect leek for planting out should be about the size of an average pencil. For these 'big' leeks, I usually plant them out just under a foot apart. Don't simply yank them out of the pot - tip the whole thing out onto your hand and shake the root ball apart, carefully teasing apart the roots. There is an art to planting leeks. Before you plant them, trim off about a quarter of the tops - simply hold the bunch of plants in one hand and cut off the tops - ensure this is well above the hidden growing point. Trim the roots so they are about half an inch long. Now use your dibber, make a neat hole by twisting it in and out about two thirds of the length of your leek plant. Simply push your plant in gently to the bottom of the hole, this should leave a tuft of leaves sticking up equal to about one third of the overall length of your plant. DO NOT FILL THE HOLE IN. When you have a plant in each hole, carefully fill each hole nearly to the top with water, trying not to knock too much earth in. In a perfect world this will fill the hole about a quarter full of earth, it is nothing to worry about if, as is usual, more falls in, it is just an 'ideal' to aim for. As your leeks grow, so will the weeds, it is quite important to keep on top of these by sending them to their new home, the compost heap, at regular intervals. If the weather turns dry and the moist soil is more than an inch below the surface, I allow myself the indulgence of watering these leeks. I am normally far too lazy to do such things, unless things are really bad.

As the plants grow, gradually 'earth them up'; this requires a little care. When doing this I grasp the leek in one hand at ground level, sliding my hand upwards an inch or so, this is to keep the leaves tight so soil cannot get in the leaf axil. Still holding the plant, I then push soil around the leaves to hold them there. When I have worked along the row, I can then use my hoe to draw some more soil around the row. This will eventually not only fill the remains of the trench but build up a ridge, much as you get with your potatoes. The purpose of all this faffing around is to 'blanch' as much of the leek as possible, without filling each layer of the leek with soil.

The most difficult bit with large leeks is lifting them. They develop some serious roots when grown like this; to get them out of the ground I use my spade. Push it in to its full depth on all four sides of the leek you want to eat, keeping your spade a couple of inches away from the plant so you don't damage the leek. When you have cut the last side, and your spade is still fully in the soil, gently lean it back and your leek should come out with a combination of the leverage of your spade and a gentle pull. I find the best way is to have your spade lifting across the row, so as not to disturb the next leek. I always trim my leeks over the compost heap as this saves me clearing the excess leaves and bits of root up later.

As for the rest of my leeks, I grow them in much of the same way, except I don't bother to break up the bottom of the trench, and only mix a moderate amount of sieved compost into the site, a layer of a couple of inches is enough. These are planted in exactly the same way except I space them six inches apart and, apart from watering them in, I rarely water them. I still 'earth them up' just as carefully but not as much, the final ridge is usually only a few inches high, rather than nearly a foot.

Enjoy your leeks, remember to hold them fairly tightly when you 'earth up', there is nothing worse than cutting a chunk off a leek covered with white sauce and melted butter and finding a dark, gritty ring inside!

CHAPTER SIXTEEN

BITS AND PIECES

In a previous section I mentioned something I referred to as 'catch crops'; this term covers a multitude of quick growing little bits and pieces. The classic 'catch crop' I have already mentioned - using radishes in between your little clumps of slow germinating parsnip seeds. There is no point in sowing more of such crops in a batch than you will be able to eat; if you sow radish seed in every gap in your parsnip row[s] you will waste most of your radish seed as you will not be able to eat all of them before they start to go 'wooly' in the middle. So I plant other things in some of the gaps; although I can't stand the stuff, some of my family like rocket, so a few of the gaps have a pinch of rocket sown in them. The other crop I use in this situation is 'Little Gem' lettuce; you can sow three or four seeds in the middle of each gap then thin them down to a single plant as they grow, this is fine. However, I have serious slug problems in my garden so I sow a few seeds of 'Little Gem' in a pot just after New Year in the greenhouse - you can just as easily use a windowsill. If you do, put the pot on a saucer so it doesn't make a ring on 'the Boss's' paintwork. Another little point when placing a pot in a saucer or something similar, always put a little layer of very fine gravel or grit in the bottom and stand the pot on this. If you stand your pot directly on the flat hard surface of a saucer, sooner or later you will over water it and the pot will become water logged; this is not a good thing, especially when the days are short. When the seedlings are large enough to handle safely pot them up, one in a three and a half inch pot. I do this when the first true leaf is nearly one inch long. If you do it earlier there is a real danger of damaging the plant; at this time of year any damage to these fragile leaves will almost certainly result in the plant rotting off. The other thing is to take care not to over water the seedlings. Over watering and rough handling are two sure fire ways of ruining these early seedlings. Frost can be a problem if, like me, you have no effective heater in your greenhouse. I overcome this problem with a sheet of bubble wrap; placed carefully, bubble side down, it will keep the plants safe from several degrees of frost. Just remember to take it off if the sun comes out and lifts the temperature in the greenhouse more than a degree or so above freezing. Growing these bits and pieces as early as this is a risk. Some years you may well lose most of these early plants if you don't have an effective heater. For what it is worth I think these risks are worthwhile. The seeds of the varieties I use for this are among the cheapest available, and we are only talking about a tiny fraction of those in the packet.

The first seeds I sow are 'Little Gem' lettuce and a cheap packet of rocket from the market stall or the supermarket. You are, after all, likely to lose a fair proportion of these, so why waste the better seed. To keep the seed in the open packets fresh, if they are in foil carefully roll the open end as tightly shut as you can without damaging the seed, put it back in its outer packet, roll this up and twist a rubber band round it to prevent it becoming unrolled. I keep mine in an old washed out margarine carton, lined with a bit of thick cloth to keep the light out. This is kept in a cool, dark but frost free shed; this seems to work alright as I have never had a problem.

Now, I know it is alright for me to rabbit on about sowing my seeds in this size pot, then potting them up in that size pot, using potting compost and all the other bits and pieces, I have a greenhouse, so I use it, I also have loads of pots.

One of my neighbours always grows his tomatoes in grow bags, using new ones every year, throwing out the old ones, waste not, want not. The idea of this book is to save money, not spend a small fortune. If you mix the contents of an old grow bag with an equal amount of finely sieved compost off your heap you will have a perfectly adequate mixture to grow your seedlings in. If you have to go out and buy a grow bag, get the cheapest you can find, it will still do the job.

If you haven't got any pots then the plastic cups from vending machines will, at a pinch, do the job. Two things to remember if you use these plastic cups - you must put a hole in the bottom to allow them to drain, the easiest way is to use something hot. I have seen it done with a cigarette, although I do not recommend trying to smoke the remainder afterwards. It will make the right sized hole though. I would suggest a metal rod heated in a fire, but wear a thick glove as heat travels along the metal - try a Phillips type screw driver with a wooden handle, as long as you can heat just the point.

The other point is a little more subtle. The plastic on these drinks cups is very thin and light gets through. This is not a good thing as in general roots do not like light. It is not difficult to overcome this problem, as long as the pots are touching each other the problem will be restricted to the outside pots. It is a simple matter to use a small piece of board, just enough to stop direct light striking the exposed sides, even a piece of black polythene will do the job.

If you haven't got a greenhouse you can use the kitchen windowsill to germinate your seeds, please ask the wife first! One thing to remember is if a sharp frost is forecast, either move them off the sill overnight or ensure the curtain is between them and the glass. It is safer to move them as cold air 'runs' down the glass and creeps under the curtain; this will be 'curtains' for your seedlings, and this will still happen even with double glazing for anything worse than minus two or three.

If you raise your seedlings on the window sill, you will need a cold frame to grow them on until they are large enough to plant out. This is not as difficult as it may sound; you don't have to be a reincarnation of Tommy Walsh to build an effective frame. A cheap and easy way of making one is to get an old window from a builder. A single large pane will be better than several little ones. The back of the frame needs to be higher than the front, to allow water to run off, so put the thickest part of the window frame at the top. A couple of pieces of board to seal the ends and you've cracked it. The 'walls' of your frame can be held in place with a couple of strong, short stakes on either side, simply knocked in with a hammer. It really doesn't matter if the ends stick up a bit, as long as the top sits snugly between them. What does matter is the height; you need at least six inches between the top of the pot and the glass on the low side, as a rule of thumb make the low side about a foot high, measured from the ground level. It is also a good idea to have a couple lengths of string running back to front, firmly anchored to a large nail or screw to prevent the top blowing off in a strong wind. Make this string long enough to tie off when you have the top propped up, as this is when it is most likely to catch the wind.

In the event of a frost being forecast, cover any young plants with a piece of bubble wrap, bubbles down, and don't forget to remove it when the temperature rises as the bubbles will act like a magnifying glass when the sun comes out and burn the soft leaves.

Although I don't like the things, this is one place were I would use slug killer pellets, as long as you use your trowel to pick up any dead slimy thieves and bury them in the compost heap, out of the way of anything looking for an easy meal.

As well as your 'catch' crops of lettuce, rocket and the like, you can do the same thing with spring onions; simply sow a few seeds in a pot, drinking cup, whatever, about half a dozen seeds is about right. Do not re-pot these, simply plant the clump out where you want them. Remember, water the compost before you sow your seeds, water them after you have sown them and you'll wash them all over the place. To avoid the pots drying out you can place a small sheet of glass over the top. If all of your pots are the same size then a single sheet will cover several pots. Glass has its obvious dangers so an easy alternative is to buy a roll of plastic sandwich bags, one pot per bag, easy!

Remember to keep an eye on the pots; if they dry out on the surface, use one of those cheap little mist sprayers until the seedlings are well up; by then it is time to remove the bag anyway, at least a week before transplanting. Don't forget to label your pots. I, like many other gardeners, trust to memory as to what I have sown where; an increasingly risky strategy with advancing years!

As to which varieties to grow, well the spring onion selects itself for the 'new' grower. It has to be 'White Lisbon' - cheap, tough, from the growing point of view, puts up with more than most of its kind from the weather and tastes good.

When it comes to lettuce, I suppose a lot depends on your personal tastes. As I have already suggested I sow a few seeds of 'Little Gem' very early, grow them on in pots to plant between the slow germinating parsnips - sometimes this comes off, sometimes not. Remember we are talking about a mere pinch of seeds here, so it has to be worth taking a chance.

Sometime in the second half of March, dependant as ever on the weather, I make my first sowing of my favourite 'Iceberg' type, the variety I use for these earlier sowings is called 'Saladin'. I continue to sow a few [about 10] every two weeks until middle to late May when I switch to 'Webbs' Wonderful' . I make the change then because Webbs tolerates the higher temperatures better than Saladin. For the last sowings, around the end of July, I tend to switch back, although with the lack of a crystal ball as to the weather this can and does sometimes come unstuck.

There is a disease called 'tip burn' which effects lettuce. This is where odd leaves, often within the heart of the plant, turns into a brown, disgusting layer of slime. Ugh!! It usually starts with the soft edges of leaves going grey and crispy around the centre of the plant. The usual cause of this is an excess of available nitrogen in the soil, in my case probably too much fresh compost, something I must hold my hand up to on occasions. It is more a matter of balance, getting your plants to grow as fast as possible without overdoing it, overdo it with lettuce and this is what happens.

Another type I like is 'Salad Bowl'. This is a frilly, pick and pick again type, available in green or red, fun to grow and tastes good - not to mention adding colour to the salad mix. Plant these and the 'Iceberg' types at least a foot apart; I usually grow my early Icebergs under my blackberry row; the canes above offer a degree of protection from a late radiation type frost… it works for me.

If you like the soft 'butter head' type then you will be best growing a variety called 'All the Year Round'. It won't like the extreme heat of a heat wave, we should be so lucky!!

Don't sow in the depths of winter, but established plants will stand the winter well in a sheltered spot or cold greenhouse, giving tasty lettuce as early as March. With practice you will be able to grow this one to pick almost any time of the year. This selection - Little Gem, Saladin, Webbs Wonderful, Salad bowl and Butter Head will provide a varied selection pretty well throughout the year. The trick is to keep sowing a few seeds at regular intervals so you always have some to plant in those little gaps which would otherwise be wasted space. The trick is to plant only in those gaps which would still be gaps by the time the lettuce is harvested; try to avoid planting in a gap where the lettuce will smother the slower growing plants, such as parsnips. Little Gem is the ideal variety for this situation. Equally you do not want odd, isolated plants in what would otherwise be a clear patch where you could plant another full row of something longer term.

As to which 'rocket' to grow is something I will leave to the individual. I don't care how 'good' it supposed to be, I can't stand the stuff, so it therefore follows I can't express an opinion as to which is best.

For growing, the same as lettuce seems to work well - a pinch of seed in a pot, transplant into single pots, then plant out 10 to12 inches apart or tucked into handy gaps. The little and often principle works just as well with rocket as with lettuce. I'm told by my family the plants are at their best when growing fast and tender and kept picked.

SEVENTEEN

THE CABBAGE FAMILY

If you use the combination of window sill and frame for your bits and pieces, you can also use this method for growing your brassicas, which is the next topic to deal with. Maybe this section should be called traditional brassicas as most Chinese leaves are, strictly speaking, members of the great cabbage family. I will deal with these in a separate section later in the book.

The thing about brassicas is they are, for the most part, large vigorous plants requiring a lot of space, an important consideration in a small garden. An average packet of seed is going to produce enough plants to fill a small modern garden on its own! So what to do? Some brassicas you can grow over a long period - 'Greyhound' cabbage and 'all the year round' cauliflower, are two which spring to mind. The answer with these is much the same as lettuce. Simply sow a few [10 to 15] seeds in a pot once a month from late January onwards, until late July. Pot the seedlings up, one in a three and a half inch pot, or drinks cup, then plant out about two feet apart as soon as they are big enough, after hardening off for a week in a cold frame. In practice this means sowing a fresh batch of seed when you plant the previous batch out, so it is straight forward enough to keep a continuous supply of these staple crops ready for harvest from May through to Christmas, weather permitting!

If you are a lover of coleslaw then you will no doubt want to grow your own cabbage. My favourite cabbage, 'Greyhound', for all its virtues is not good for this. To get the solid white cabbage needed I recommend another old favourite, 'Primo'; grow it the same as the other summer cabbages and cauliflowers, sowing a succession, starting in mid February, sowing the last in mid May. These later sowings will provide you with cabbages until the winter crops are ready round about Christmas time, barring any exceptionally bad weather. One other point about 'Primo', it is probably a good idea to give the plants an extra six inches of space compared to 'Greyhound' as they can get quite large if they like your soil.

Calabrese, often called green broccoli, can be grown in much the same way. Many varieties available are F1 hybrids and are therefore relatively expensive. This also means those sown together crop together, an advantage if you have a freezer and want the ground clear for another crop. This is also a disadvantage if you are growing for 'fresh', so for this reason try a variety called 'Kabuki'; these will mature over a period of a couple of weeks. Leave the plants after you have cut the central 'head' and a couple of weeks or so later you will get a second crop of tasty side shoots. The effect of this is it will be about a month, may be a little more, from cutting your first 'head' to the last feed of side shoots, by which time the next batch should be ready.

If you want to grow a batch for your freezer, then try a variety called 'Zen'. This is an F1 with a high resistance to many common diseases. As always there is a sneaky little tip - sow the seed the day you lift your first roots of early potatoes, sow these in a small seed tray rather than a pot. A silver foil tray, at least 3inches deep will do, the sort some super- markets sell small pre-packet roasting joints in will be just fine; remember to make several holes in the bottom with a nail to allow for drainage.

Pot the seedlings up as soon as they are big enough to handle, this is when they have their first true leaf about an inch long.

Get it right and your plants will be perfect to plant out when you lift the last of your earliest row of potatoes. Ideally these should be planted 2 feet apart with 2 feet between the rows, however, as the intention is a quick crop for the freezer, then plant them a little closer, cut the spacing down to eighteen inches. To compensate for this closer spacing, plant the second row opposite to the gaps in the first, there should easily be room for two rows of calabrese following a row of 'spuds'.

Most of the remaining varieties of brassicas are types which either over winter as substantial plants or are actually for winter harvest. There is however one other type which crops in the autumn which is worthy of a few notes before we move on to the winter crops. In recent years Romanesco has become increasingly popular, and with good reason; some class it as a calabrese others as a broccoli, it is best described as a slightly yellowish, pointed cauliflower. From the eating point of view it has more or at least a stronger flavour than a cauliflower; it is great simply steamed and tossed in butter, but in a cauliflower cheese it is superb. After cutting the main head, leave the plant and you will get another tasty crop a few weeks later, in much the same way as with sprouting broccoli. As excellent as I find Romanesco there is a drawback, the plants can get huge. If they really like your soil then three feet apart is hardly enough, something to be borne in mind before opting to grow it.

I sow a few seeds in a pot in early March, then pot up as soon as the seedlings are large enough, the first true leaf stage, as with the calabrese. If the weather has been mild I might well yield to the temptation and make a sowing a couple of weeks earlier, then follow up with a second sowing at the end of March, but then I am lucky, I have a greenhouse and a large garden.

With so many different brassicas in pots at the same time it becomes very important to label them. If you do not, it is a certainty mix ups will occur leading to a degree of inconvenience with cabbages growing where the calabrese should have been.

So, to the winter crops - the classic is the humble, often maligned brussels sprout. Most people will be looking for a good crop of hard buttons ready for Christmas. With this in mind it is worth taking a little care in selecting which variety to grow. Times were when there was little choice, now it can get a bit confusing with some varieties maturing as early as September, others will not be ready until March. Of the multitude of varieties available, the best, in my opinion, is one called 'Clodius', remember we are looking for the perfect Christmas sprout.

As with most things there is a drawback to growing this variety. It is an F1 and at near enough five pence per seed it goes against the main aim of this book, which is to save money. That said, I have found this to be the best Christmas cropper I have grown. If most of the 50 or so seeds grow then you will have far too many plants for an average garden as these things need to be a minimum of 2 feet apart, ideally a little more. So what to do? You can, of course buy a few plants, saving seed until next year isn't really an option, some may well grow but they will have lost much of their vigour. Why not form a loose co-operative with three or four friends or family; if one of you has a greenhouse use that to provide the group with plants. The same system will work for so many crops and will reduce your costs as many packets of seed will produce far more plants than today's relatively small gardens can cope with. You can, if you have the greenhouse, of course sell your excess plants to your neighbours; you should at least get the cost of your seeds back.

Buying 'plug' plants is becoming increasingly popular and has its advantages, but you only have to lose a few plants to slugs, collared doves whatever, and it would have been cheaper to have bought your vegetables at the supermarket. However, if you do not have the time, or have trouble raising seedlings for whatever reason, then the plant option is worth considering.

One thing with 'spouts', more so than most other brassicas, is the need for firm soil! On all but the heaviest of clays, tread it down well after digging, using the 'shuffle' described earlier. It won't hurt to go over the patch twice on light soils. If your soil is too light and fertile there is a good chance of your hard won sprouts ending up more like mini cabbages than firm sprouts, this is referred to as 'blowing'. It is also worth remembering the tops of sprout plants, once you have picked all the sprouts, make a useful 'green' in their own right, not unlike spring cabbage.

Another good variety is one called 'United'. This is a heavy cropper, with large sprouts and good flavour. However, even sowing in April, mine have always been well past their best by Christmas. 'Clodius' on the other hand, sown at the same time, are at their peak for the festive season. I find the first or second week in April to be ideal; this will not necessarily be the perfect time where you are, only by trial and error will you find the optimum timing for your own particular patch.

Another crop worth considering, if you have the room, is sprouting broccoli; the requirements are similar to sprouts. Personally I only grow the purple type. As I grow winter cauliflowers I do not see the need to grow the white variety. There is an old, cheap, tried and trusted variety usually sold as 'Early Purple Sprouting'. Not exactly an original name, it is however accurate; sown at the same time as your sprouts and planted out late May to early June, it will yield masses of tasty shoots just at the time when fresh vegetables are in relatively short supply. The best thing about this crop is it comes again after your first picking; with a little care and luck most years you can even get a third picking, just before you need to clear the ground for your next crop.

Again, a single packet of seed will produce far more plants than you will ever need. For the first time grower, plant them a generous 2 feet apart. Once you have got the hang of things and your soil into good condition, you will soon find you need to give them a bit more room; on really good soil and sown at the ideal time even 3 feet is hardly enough, but it does take a bit of practice to get this just right. Another good point in favour of growing this crop is it does not matter if too much comes at any one time; it is a simple matter to blanch what you cannot eat and freeze the excess for future use.

I mentioned winter cauliflowers - these are one of my favourites. The variety I grow is not surprisingly an old one, 'Vietches' self protecting'. As the name suggests, its leaves curl over the creamy-white curd protecting the good bit from the worst excesses of our winter weather. It is one of the most reliable varieties of any vegetable which I have grown. Sown in the greenhouse in mid to late April, potted up as soon as they are large enough to handle, the plants are usually ready to plant out around the end of June or the first week in July. This is pretty well perfect to follow an early [over wintered] row of peas or the over wintered broad beans. If you are able to get the timing just right with this you will have cracking cauliflowers from around Christmas time, right through until the first signs of spring. A prolonged cold spell will slow things down somewhat, but a few warm days will normally bring on a few plants so they are ready to cut.

About the only crop of the conventional 'winter greens' left to cover are the winter cabbages and savoys. Savoys are little more than cabbages with heavily crinkled leaves; whether you grow these or the more conventional 'January King' is down to personal choice.

Cultivation is much the same as most other winter 'greens'; sow from mid April through to late May, potting the seedlings up when big enough to handle, exactly the same as all the others in this group. The reasons for the two sowings, one early, the other late is firstly to allow me to extend the cropping season of some of the most useful vegetables available at this time of year; the other is so I have a little flexibility to cope with our unpredictable weather. Should one batch be checked by unseasonable weather, then there is a good chance the other batch will be alright, at least that is the thinking behind the two sowings. As far as spacing is concerned, two feet apart, both between plants and between rows is about right except for one or two particularly large varieties.

All that remains to be said is, remember, all these brassicas prefer firm soil. They will also do better on the heavier soils than light sandy soil. I have already dealt with pests and diseases earlier; in a small garden it may be worthwhile covering your 'greens' with a muslin net to keep off the ravenous hordes of large white butterflies. Net curtains will work quite well up to a point, but please remember to ask the wife first!

Don't forget the 'earthing up' tip, cabbages and their cousins have big leaves and catch a lot of wind, so it is important they have the extra support this provides, and of course this 'earthing up' also makes life much more difficult for the cabbage root fly to lay their eggs on the actual root. It could well be the case this earthing up I am so keen on, is much more beneficial by filling in the inevitable gap around the stem thus making life difficult for the cabbage root fly than it is for helping support the plant - all I know is it definitely makes a difference.

And finally, when it comes time to clear your crop, don't get all macho and grab a cut off sprout stem and give it a yank, not unless you want a week or so off work flat on your back!

These things generally have tough roots; on lighter soils such as mine shoving a fork under the roots, more or less horizontal, a couple of inches down, then lifting, using your legs, NOT your back, will, if the stem is against the end of the handle, usually remove the old root without drama. On heavy clay soils it is a good idea to cut the roots on one or two sides with a spade before trying to get it out of the soil with your fork - a large 'Romanesco' or sprouting broccoli can take a bit of shifting, so take care. Before I throw this sort of material onto the compost heap, I always chop it up with my spade, especially the hard stems. Do this on a firm patch of soil, not on the patio or paving slabs. Chopping on concrete is a bad idea, it will not only chip the slabs but ruin your spade!

I know I said at the outset I was going to try to write this in the order things needed doing. Okay, I digressed, but it seemed easier to cover all the traditional brassicas together, as it is only the timing which differs one to another.

CHAPTER EIGHTEEN

POTATOES

So to get back on track I will now deal with the humble spud!

Right at the outset let me say it will be the exception rather than the rule to get any amount of large potatoes from a crop in your garden. Commercial growers use a lot of fertilizer and water heavily to produce the relatively large tubers you buy in the supermarket. Normally there is little point in growing maincrop potatoes in a garden, they take up a lot of space, and simply are not worth the hassel of the work and storing them. That said there is no better crop to help 'clean up' a patch of ground being planted for the first time.

We are getting ahead of ourselves again. To start with I will deal with growing some early potatoes - even in a small garden it is worth growing a few of these. The flavour of a feed of early spuds, fresh from the garden, can never be equalled by any shop bought ones, organic or otherwise.

When you plant these of course depends on where you live and the weather, but in general you should be looking to get the first row in in early March. I have even got away with planting a row in late February when the weather has been on my side. One thing you can count on, this first row will get their tops cut by frost, it will check them but will not kill them as long as you have kept them well earthed up.

If ever there is a crop where the ability to dig matters, then this is it. I have seen all manner of 'dodges' for planting potatoes, but at the end of the day the method I am going to describe will produce the most consistent results in almost any situation.

Let's deal with some of the 'dodges' first; the commonest one is to simply push your 'seed' into the ground along a line then 'earth' them up straight away. Fine, it is quick and easy, as long as your soil has already been dug. The down side is you will most likely break off some of the shoots, and the more shoots you have, the more potatoes you will get, and this is all about numbers, not size! The biggest down side is your plants will be shallow and susceptible to drought, which in turn will mean more 'scabs' on your tubers, which are also likely to be smaller than you hoped for.

Another fairly commonly used 'dodge' is to take out a shallow trench with your hoe and plant your 'spuds' in the trench before earthing them up. Again they will be susceptible to the effects of drought.

There is another side effect of these shallow planting methods - the side roots which produce your crop grow from the shoots which become the visible part of the plant, and always above the tuber you planted. If your tubers are only planted a few inches deep then there is only an inch or two from which your crop can grow. Having said all this, there maybe the odd occasion when planting in a shallow trench is a worthwhile option. If your soil is heavy and poorly drained with a shallow top soil, this method may be worth a try, with the proviso you add an inch or two of fine [sifted] compost and hoe it into the bottom of your trench.

There is a growing trend to grow potatoes, especially earlies, in all manner of containers - anything from none too large pots to industrial aggregate bags, which need a forklift to shift them. Why? It costs a fortune to grow them this way, and this book is supposed to be about growing decent veg on the cheap. Fair enough if you only have a patio, or small courtyard garden and you really love new spuds. If you want to try it, then fine - if you have one of those half barrels which usually have gaudy annuals in them, try that. Use the compost which grew last years bizzie-lizzies and lobelias, tip the old compost out on the paving slabs and mix the contents of a new growbag with it. Refill your tub and plant four to six potatoes in it, obviously depending on the size of the tub. There is no need to plant them too deep, about eight inches will do.

One advantage of this is you can start them off in a conservatory or the greenhouse, moving it outside when the risk of frost has past. Remember though, these will be very tender, even a strong breeze can 'scorch' the leaves and if the night time temperature drops to within three or even four degrees of freezing you can still get a radiation frost on a calm, clear night. With all this in mind, there is no point in planting before mid February. Of course you can plant some just after Christmas, and you will get a few very early potatoes, but grown inside the tops will become rank and straggle all over the place due to the low light at this time of year. The question has to be asked, is it worth it for a hand full of spuds the size of pheasant eggs, at best only a week or so before the first outdoor crop? Maybe, if only to get one over on the clever old sod [me] just up the road by claiming the bragging rights for the first spuds in the street.

Many of you will have heard the term 'chitting your seed'. This is not some strange tribal ritual making a sacrifice to the weather gods, it is the process of getting your potatoes to produce shoots before they are planted. There are two common mistakes made when attempting this - the first is to keep your 'seed' in the dark for too long, this results in fragile, long white shoots which will always break off, often under their own weight. Clearly, this is not good. The other mistake is to simply spread your seed in a tray, any which way up. A little trick I learned from Jersey growers many years ago, is to stand your seed tubers on end in a tray. If you look at a potato, you will see sunken buds called eyes - there will be more at one end than at the other. Put the end with the most eyes upper most; if you can, pack them in just tight enough so they can't move about if the tray is tipped. In fact an easy way of doing this is to tip the tray towards you. I find standing the back edge on a brick works just fine; by tipping the tray like this it helps to stop the first ones rolling around too much.

Once you have your tray of seed packed nicely in, stand it on the greenhouse bench on a piece of bubble wrap, large enough to totally wrap the entire tray, bubbles inwards. If you can, stand your tray on a couple of thin pieces of wood or garden cane cut to the width of the tray, then it will not squash all the bubbles underneath.

It is probably a good idea to wrap it up for a few days, may be a week or so; as ever it depends on the weather. When you can see the shoots beginning to grow, then it is time to unwrap the tray. Leave it on the bubble wrap as you will need to wrap it up again if a frost is possible, even a slight frost can get the shoots, greenhouse or not. If more than two degrees of frost are forecast then add another sheet of bubble wrap on top, again bubbles on the inside. I am assuming you have no heat in your greenhouse or conservatory, or at best only a very little. The aim of all this is to have nicely 'chitted seed' when you want to plant them, the ideal shoot is just under an inch long and green, not white. To achieve this your seed need to be fairly cool, but frost free, and above all have plenty of light. It may even be worth while putting an artificial light over them for three hours or so every evening. Do not use an old tungsten bulb as this produces mainly 'red' light which is useless on potatoes - the ideal would be a small fluorescent tube. These produce mainly blue light which is what all plants in the potato family use. You can use the same light later on to help your young tomato plants. One other little point is dirty glass stops more 'blue' light than it does red, so clean glass matters quite a lot. You might get the feeling that a greenhouse with dirty glass seems warmer. This is why,our eyes see red and blue light, red 'feels' warmer, the accumulated crud stops a lot of the blue, and blue 'feels' colder, it is quite literally all in the mind.

When you start digging to plant your potatoes, remember to put your line in, at least two and a half feet from the edge of your plot, or if you are planting next to another crop, leave at least three feet. Remember this is not a contest to lift the biggest spade full! Take your time and do it right. Try to keep your rows of digging fairly straight; when you have one row left, about six inches, use your line as a guide to get this last trench straight and even. Now is a good time to move your line, but as we are only planting one row for now, it is important to mark where you pulled it up from, as well as a small stick at the end of the row of 'seed' potatoes. This may sound like overkill but think about it, when you come to plant your next row of 'proper' earlies and you measure from the sticks at the end of the row of 'seed' then your next row will be too close. I know, I've done it! Well I am getting 'old' according to my 'kids', grand or otherwise. The other reason for getting your line out of the way is you will probably bury it adding the compost; failing that you are almost certain to trip over it, probably while pushing your wheelbarrow. I've done that too! OUCH! [or something similar].

Remember we are talking about what is really a speculative row.

It really is taking a chance in most areas planting a row of spuds, even in early March. There is little point in wasting money on expensive 'seed' for this row, equally there is no point in using a lot of compost, an inch or two of sieved compost is sufficient. Spread this along the trench fairly evenly and 'scratch' it in with your fork; you will find it easier if you have your fork at about 45 degrees to the line of your trench, keeping the handle straight up. If you have got this right then the bottom of your trench will be fairly flat and near enough level, with about three inches of fine, soft soil mixed with the compost.

Get your tray of 'chitted' seed and push them gently into the bottom of your prepared trench; take care to get the shoots pointing upwards. Try to get them at an even depth and as near to straight up the middle of your trench as you can and about a foot apart. Do not plant them too close to the undug side, for reasons I will explain in a moment. One other little tip - if, as often happens you have just got your trench ready to plant and O.C. Domestics [the wife] calls you in with a request for 'can you just' or 'we have got to pop over to..' remember to put your seed back under cover. This always happens on a nice sunny day. Leave them out and after the 'popping over to' etc it will no doubt be dark on your return and you WILL forget you left them out, and at this time of year sunny days are usually followed by night frost! Remember what I said about 'radiation' frosts? Such things as a tray of 'chitted' seed spuds left out in the open is a prime target.

By the time you get back to planting your spuds the soil in your trench will probably have dried out, at least on the surface. This may be no bad thing as it will also have warmed up a bit. As this usually happens to me I have found it a good idea to 'scratch' the bottom of the trench again, but very lightly, about an inch deep should be about right.

So, at last we have a row of potatoes, nice and straight along the middle of your trench, shoots pointing upwards, ready to be buried; don't forget the little marker sticks, put them in now, in line with the potatoes.

Now for another 'sneaky tip'; when you do your first row of digging to cover them up, turn side ways on to your trench, so your spade, or fork, is at right angles to your trench, and turn your 'spit' sideways onto your 'seed'. Obviously you take small 'spits' as dumping a massive lump of earth onto them will break off the shoots; with a bit of care and practice you will still be able to keep things level.

Why bother? Well, if you dig normally then when you lean your spade, or fork, backwards the bottom will come up under, or nearly under your 'seed'. You must take small 'spits' for this row, so you don't break the shoots. Taking small 'spits' makes this under cutting inevitable, with the result much of the loose soil/compost mix falls into the bottom of your new trench, probably bringing some of your 'seed' with it. The net result is a higgledy-piggledy row, as straight as a dog's hind leg. The 'seed' which fell out of their soft bed don't poke their heads up until the earliest are a foot high, hardly surprising as they end up nearly a foot deep and probably upside down. Hence the ninety degree turn in digging, obvious? I forget how many years my potato rows were crooked and uneven before I realised what was happening! This little trick also helps in another way: when you plant the rest of your 'spuds' we want to get as much compost in as possible. Digging this row at right angles tends to leave a slightly larger trench, which will hold extra compost right where we want it, next to the plants; in fact I tend to do the same thing on the row before the planting trench. By putting the compost next to the plants as well as the sieved stuff in the planting trench, it is in easy reach of the plants. There is also the added bonus you don't hoe it up when earthing up the crop which is the main reason I don't put any in the intermediate rows of digging.

Planting your 'proper' crop of earlies simply follow the same method; you can get away with planting the rows two and a half feet apart if your digging technique is good, otherwise leave three feet to be safe. The other thing is don't plant all your earlies at the same time, if you do then the last ones will have begun to harden before you use them, rather defeating the purpose of growing them.

Depending on the length of your rows and your consumption, try to work out how long it will take you to eat the first row. We'll say a week for argument's sake - then plant your rows one a week. Simple?? Whether or not you took a chance on a 'silly' early row, around the end of March is a good time to start planting in most areas, with all the usual provisos regarding weather and soil etc.

There are many varieties to choose from, and in all honesty much of what governs your choice will be down to personal taste as well as location. All I can do is to say my favourite is a variety called 'Nadine'. Strictly speaking this is what is known as a 'second early', in other words it will take about a couple of weeks longer from planting to harvest than a true early. But I like 'Nadine'; in my opinion it is the finest eating of all the potatoes grown to eat 'fresh' - others are ready to eat quicker, many crop heavier, but none match that 'new' potato flavour - this is of course just my opinion.

Main Crop Potatoes

Main crops are the varieties which are grown to store. Unless you have a very large garden there is not much point in growing them as you can buy 25kg for a fiver. However, if you decide to grow a couple of rows then fair enough.

The choice of which variety to grow has to be governed by personal taste, and to some extent how yours are usually cooked. If you like 'roasties' then it is difficult to beat 'Maris Piper'; on the other hand if your family are chip addicts then the old favourite 'King Edward' maybe the best bet. One of my personal favourites is the red skinned 'Desiree'; it crops well, is alright for 'roasties', makes passable chips and is great for mash; the big ones bake well and it is not bad when lifted as an early. Against it, some other varieties resist drought better and when blight is about you can be certain it will be one of the first to get it, but careful crop husbandry will usually get you a decent crop.

It is a good idea to plant these away from your tomatoes, as far away as your rotation will allow, the reason being tomatoes will get the same blight which always affects potatoes to some extent. As your main crop spuds will be in the ground until the tops die off, they are likely to infect your tomatoes just as they are reaching their peak, which is a wholly undesirable state of affairs. Many of the green tomatoes will ripen inside, weeks after the first frosts, add blight into the equation and most of these will go black and rot instead of red. So keep these main crop spuds away from the tomatoes.

These main crop potatoes will need more compost than their early counterparts, as they are in the ground longer and hopefully get bigger. Obviously there is a limit to how much compost can be dug in close to the 'seed', and as I have already said there is little point in digging compost in mid-way between the rows as this gets in the way when earthing up.

Plant these exactly the same as your early potatoes, with a generous three feet between the rows. If the weather is alright then early April is a good time to plant. If things are good soil and weather wise and you live south of the Humber then you might well get away with planting in the third week of March, though this will usually mean the tops will get 'cut' by frost at least once. In itself unwelcome, but it need not be a disaster - if a frost, or even temperatures of three or four are forecast, nip out with the hoe and earth your spuds up, to the extent most are covered with soil, inevitably odd leaves will still stick out. If you only have a few then as well as the extra earthing up, cover them with a bit of 'fleece' or bubble wrap; don't forget to weight the edges down with an odd brick or piece of pipe. Another little tip, if you do use fleece or bubble wrap, put a few supports under it to keep it off the leaves - a couple of odd pieces of wood nailed together in a 't' shape is all that is needed.

There is no need to go mad with this, a gap of an inch will do, then if the temperature does drop an extra degree or so your spuds will survive, not 'tweeked' by the frost or scorched by the sun; the condensation drops on the underside of your frost cover will act like a magnifying glass for the sun's rays.

If potatoes will grow out of a slight freezing of their leaves and upper stems, with no obvious damage visible after a couple of weeks, and the effect on the eventual crop will be negligible, unless the damage was severe, why bother? Now this will not happen every year, but you can be sure, the year you grow some potatoes, and plant them a little earlier to get one over on your uncle along the road, or the neighbour, an unexpected frost 'cuts' one or two of your most forward plants, but they grow out of it just fine, as spuds do. A month or so later, during a warm, wet spell, your plants begin to look sick, just an odd brown-grey leaf, on the very plants which got 'cut'. You may not even notice the first ones as they are usually hidden in the middle of the plant; before you know it most of the row are looking rather poorly. Odds are this is the dreaded blight, it is going to happen anyway, but yours have got it first and you have lost two or three weeks during which time your crop would have doubled had the tops stayed healthy, like Mr. Cautious's next door! This is all down to frost damage; it has left some dead tissue, and the blight gets a head start and reduces your crop - this is the only reason it is worth protecting your main crop potatoes. With the earlies, that is those which are to be lifted while the tops are still green to eat as new potatoes, it really makes little difference, and simply earthing up will suffice.

A little way back I said about the need for extra compost on main crop potatoes; they also need plenty of moisture. If they get dry then your crop will be greatly reduced, not to mention covered with unsightly 'scab'.

The trick is to keep them growing as long as possible, before blight rears its ugly head. Now, generally I am not an advocate of sloshing water around, get the soil right and generally it will do little good, however, main crop potatoes are one crop which will really benefit. Again there are a couple of things you can do to maximise the effect of a little water - rather than simply earthing up with soil pulled up with your hoe, try this way, it is a bit of 'messing about' but it works.

It is the weekend, and your 'spuds' are doing nicely, you are going to earth them up, there is still plenty of bare soil between the rows - get a barrow load of sifted compost ready, if it is dry then water it a little, we want it to be nicely moist, not sopping wet. Now get a watering can, or hose and water along the row of potatoes. Do it gently and slowly so it soaks into the ground around the plants; don't spray it about, most of it will be wasted and do no good at all. Having watered your row, now get your barrow load of sifted

MOIST compost, wheel it to the end of your row and tip out a small heap, being careful not to bury your plants. If you twist your barrow on the wheel guard when you tip it, you will find it easier, now walk backwards, pulling the barrow and repeat.

Use your rake, upside down, and pull the compost level, you can also carefully push some under the leaves of your plants. When you have got to the end of the row with your compost you can now earth up. Aim at getting two layers, the first of compost, then go a little deeper so you drag up a thin layer of soil which covers most of the compost.

I can hear you now, 'What a lot of b... messing about. Why?'

In the words of the meerkat on the advert, 'simple'!

The water you carefully poured along the row has soaked down to the roots, which is where we wanted it; the moist compost will help to keep the ground cool and reduce evaporation, as well as adding a little nutrient. The final thin layer of soil is to keep everything in place.

On light soils, if you get a shower of rain after a couple of dry sunny days, get out there and lightly earth up your potatoes, even if they don't really need it, again this is to aid moisture conservation. The earth you pulled up will no doubt dry out in a couple of hours of sun and breeze, the soil you covered up will not!

One other little thing I do is when I have finished an earthing up session, I always hoe between the rows. There is a bit of a 'knack' to getting the desired result. What I do is hoe a couple of feet at a time, so I start hoeing a couple of feet from the end of the row and work to the end, move back a couple of feet, and starting near my feet, work away from my feet until I reach the freshly hoed stretch. By walking backwards and repeating the process I end up with a nicely hoed strip of level, loose soil between the rows with no clonking great hoof prints on it.

There is another way of achieving the same effect and that is to reach over one row, hoeing the gap the other side as you go, much as with earthing up. For me the problem is you are twisting a little doing this, more so than when earthing up, and to put not too fine a point on it, my back is not keen on this at all.

Yet another way is if you happen to have a three tined cultivator, then you can use this as long as you are careful not to dig it in too deeply.

The other question which will arise is when do you stop earthing up? The end result should be a 'V' shaped trench between the rows, with a slight dip along the centre of the ridge where the stems of the plants come out of the ground. This is quite important as this little dip will not only help to catch any rain and allow it to soak in where it will do the most good , but will do the same for any water you add with a watering can or a gently running hose. Which ever method you use, the important thing is to do it gently; don't try to put too much water on too quickly; avoid overfilling this little trough, as this will wash soil away off the ridge, which is not what we want. It is equally important not to splash soil onto the plants, as this is the source of most diseases which can affect your crop. I know farmers use rain guns to irrigate their crops heavily, but they also spray with fungicides on a weekly basis - if they didn't then their crops would be riddled with all manner of diseases. As with most things, growing spuds is a trade off - they need moist conditions to produce good crops, moisture also enables diseases such as blight to flourish - too dry and you have a poor crop and those you do dig up will be covered with scab. It is almost inevitable you will get some scab; it might not look very nice, and badly infected tubers will not keep well, they are however still perfectly edible once peeled. So getting the balance right with any watering is an important part of growing main crop potatoes.

The reason for 'earthing up' is simple. Any tubers exposed to the light go green! These not only taste absolutely horrible, they are also slightly poisonous, so don't eat them! You can of course put any green tubers aside as seed for next year. If you do, keep a careful eye on them as they are more likely to be carrying disease then buried tubers - any sign of disease then put them in the bin, rather than the compost heap.

Keep an eye open for the 'fruits' which follow the flowers - these look like green tomatoes. These too are poisonous so keep them away from the kiddies. It is nothing to worry about as they taste horrendous, the worst that can happen is belly ache, it is just something to be aware of.

Another vexed question is just when to cut the tops off; this is a matter of judgement for the individual. The best advice I can give is leave them until only a few green leaves remain. I know this is vague, but it is difficult to be precise, as the timing depends on why the tops are dying off. It is inevitable you will get some blight. If blight is the principle cause of the tops [which are called haulm] dying, then it is as well to cut them off a bit earlier, say when about half of them are dying. If it is mainly drought and old age, then they can be left until there are only a few green leaves.

I use secateurs to cut the tops off. I usually leave about four or five inches sticking up above the ground, these are left to totally dry out. It might sound silly, but it is a good idea to lightly earth up the ridges as soon as you have raked off all the rubbish and consigned it to the compost heap along with any weeds big enough to get hold of to pull up. The reason for earthing up at this stage is as always simple - the actions of removing the tops and generally tidying up will disturb the soil in the ridges, a potato tuber does not have to be totally exposed to daylight to turn green; it may appear alright when lifted, but this is how some get that nasty 'earthy' taste. When earthing up do not completely cover the cut off stems, leave a couple of inches sticking up. These will act as markers as to the position of the roots when it comes to digging them up.

It is important not to dig main crop potatoes up too soon, they must be left until the skins have properly set. This is where the old stems again come in useful; when these are completely dead they pull up very easily. There should be no resistance from still attached roots when you pull one up; this is a good indication the skins on the potatoes have set.

Now your 'spuds' are ready to lift, pick a dry day to dig them up, a bit of breeze along with some sun will help in the vital drying process.

Using your fork, start about a foot away from the first root, right on the edge of the garden; go down as near to straight down as possible and as deep as you can sensibly go before you try to lift the soil. This is important; if you get too close you will spike or scrape your potatoes, damaged tubers will not keep. Shake out each fork full two or three times, especially on light soils, it is surprising how many quite large potatoes you can miss the first time.

Take your time and work along the row, leaving the crop in a neat row behind you. I always keep my wheelbarrow handy and throw any rubbish straight in - the old tops, stray bits of bindweed and the like, all this can go onto the compost heap. This saves picking it all up again; why move it twice? Told you I was lazy!

Old gardeners always told me to dig up my potatoes in the morning, it seemed just another 'old wives tale' at the time. Now I know why they used to do it; they wouldn't dig any up after their lunch break - the first job after lunch was to turn all those they had lifted in the morning, thus ensuring the skins dried evenly.

They would then disappear into the area of the cold frames and spend half an hour or so watering young cabbage and cauliflower plants, the types which would over winter to give you your early crops, at the same time selecting the best plants.

By the time they got back to the potato plot the tubers would be nice and dry.

I pick those to eat straight into an old paper potato sack, saved from some I had bought the previous year. When I have collected all the 'keepers', I will then select the best of the rest for seed. As I know how many I need per row it is a simple matter to select just enough, always add a few extras, one extra for every ten required is a good 'rule of thumb'. The 'perfect seed' potato is about the size of a chicken egg, with plenty of 'eyes', and is best stored in a tray in a cool, frost free, dry place; if you do store them in the dark, check them regularly; if they start to shoot bring them into the light, if you leave them they will develop long, straggly shoots.

Having selected your 'seed' you are now left with the 'splits', ones you have spiked. I told you to take your time! As long as there is a decent piece which is okay, then pick them out for immediate use, they will still taste the same.

What to do with all the little ones is always a problem. O. C. Domestics is unlikely to be impressed with the gift of a bucket full of marbles to peel. My 'boss', being the Yorkshire lass she is, found a gadget which scrubs all these 'tiddlers' clean. She then boils them until nearly ready, then drains them off, and leaves them to dry off. I'm told this is important, because she then pops them into the deep fat fryer until they are golden brown and crispy on the outside, delicious! Drying them off stops the fat exploding everywhere apparently, like I'd know! They do taste very good though.

If your good lady isn't as accommodating and either you or your neighbours have chickens, then all the badly spiked spuds, little ones and the green ones not kept for seed can be boiled up for the chooks as they are - let them cool, add any old bread and scraps, they will love them.

Having cleared your crop, rake the patch level, at the same time removing stray roots and any other bits of rubbish, of course adding it to the compost heap. Earlier I described the 'shuffle' to firm the soil. Having levelled the patch, now firm it down using the same technique, rake it again to get it nice and level. Using your line to keep the rows straight and your trowel to plant them, get your over wintering cabbage and cauliflowers planted - the ones which were watered while your potatoes were drying. Water them in, water gently around each plant, not spray them over, this is next to useless, not to mention a waste. The last job of the day was to hoe the plot drawing about half an inch of soil around the new plants, covering up the wet soil around the base of each new plant, preventing evaporation.

Those old gardeners knew a thing or two - don't work hard, work smart!! To them timing was everything… lift potatoes in the morning and by the time they 'knocked off' the potato plot had become a cabbage patch, they'd had an easy afternoon but 'the master' thought they had been 'busting a gut' all day - see if the same trick will con your 'boss'. I doubt it, but it is worth a try; you never know, she might even scrub some of the small potatoes clean and deep fry them out of sympathy!

Just remember, you will not get the uniform potatoes you buy from the supermarket, and most of the time yours are likely to be smaller on average, but they will taste a whole lot better.

CHAPTER NINETEEN

TOMATOES

This is where I upset the seed firms! I never grow my own plants, I always buy half a dozen from a local market trader who is a nurseryman as well, why? Many reasons - to grow decent tomato plants is a specialist job. What I am going to say applies to all except a very few varieties, because as with everything else there are a couple of exceptions, in this case a couple of outdoor bush varieties.

To grow good tomato plants, large enough, early enough, requires heat, not just frost protection, but real, controlled heat. Plants grown from seed which had germinated at temperatures below about 70 degrees in the old scale [Fahrenheit] will turn out to be what are known as 'jack' plants. What this means is the bottom trusses will be useless, you might get an odd fruit on them, notice I said might! Even if you can maintain the required temperatures, not difficult with an electric propagator, your plants will still end up soft and thin.

This is caused by the low natural light levels this early in the year, as the ideal time to sow is late January. Again this problem is surmountable, a small fluorescent tube about 18 inches above the plants will solve the problem, if you run it for about 6 hours a day if it is sunny or 13 hours if it's dull.

Once the plants are about an inch or so high, with the first true leaves showing clearly, it is time to pot them up, one to a 31/2 inch pot filled with a good proprietary compost. The temperature can now be dropped to about 60 at night and 68 by day, under the lights.

Even with all this messing about most of the plants will still be soft and will have weak stems. As a guide we are looking for plants which will have about 10 leaves when a foot high, and will stand alone at this height - growing good plants like this is an art form and best left to those who do it for a living!

Sure, almost anyone, even me, can grow tomatoes from seed and get a few tasty fruits, but why bother? Plants cost about 50p each! 6 will feed the biggest family, and half the street!! You see my point? Remember we are talking about growing outdoor tomatoes, grown in the ground. The 'fashion' is to grow them in grow bags. WHY? To have any chance of a decent crop you first need a large and expensive grow bag. What happens if you go away for a few days? Even with a good quality bag the plants will still need regular watering and feeding, they only have to get dry once and all your work goes up the creek and it is all too easy to over water which is as bad. I do hope all this hadn't put you off, because it really isn't difficult to grow tomatoes which are the envy of the street. I have seen it written that tomato plants have two different types of roots, the shallow 'feeding' roots and the deep ones which draw up the water- this is probably true if you are always sloshing water and feed around.

Enough of what not to do! The first thing to do is to prepare your row. Select a good sunny spot, well away from any main crop potatoes you may be growing [remember blight]. My row is usually about 12 feet long, enough for six plants. I have a large family who all like tomatoes!

The first task is to dig out a trench, two spades wide and the depth of the spade; leave the 'spoil' in two neat rounded banks on either side Break up the bottom of the trench with your fork, as deep as you can reasonably go. It is what we add to this trench which will make the difference. First of all I add a couple of barrow loads of compost, this is not normally sieved, I just shake it out with a fork to remove the biggest pieces which I throw onto the new heap. Roughly level this out with your fork and dig it into the bottom of your trench as deeply as you can; tread this down, using 'the shuffle', now add a barrow load of farmyard manure or a couple of bags of horse manure if you can get either. If not don't worry, almost fill your trench with the best sieved compost you have then dig your trench again.

The ideal time to do this is late March or early April, choosing a nice day to do it, of course. This is about a week, maybe two weeks before I buy my plants as I have no heating in my greenhouse. This is why I wait until mid April to get my plants as it is not unusual to get a quite sharp radiation frost at this time of year.

These plants are usually in a 31/2 inch pot when I get them. The first job is to re-pot them into a 1 litre pot. I simply use sieved compost for this, plant them so the top of the original compost is just covered with the new compost. A word of caution, as good as sieved compost is when used in pots, it can dry out very quickly. There is a way to reduce this problem - if you have an old grow bag, mix this in equal parts with some of your best compost and all should be well.

As I said, watch the watering. The trick is to keep things just nicely moist, never over water, this can be fatal at this time of year as the soil/compost will be quite cold. As soon as you see the first flower showing the tiniest bit of yellow give them their first weak feed, half of what it says on the packet or bottle will be more than enough. It is important to avoid splashing it onto the plants, never feed if the compost is dry. If it is then water first, just a little! Leave for a couple of hours before feeding. I tend to feed and water on alternate days, obviously only adding liquid if it is needed. I keep this up until early to mid May; the weather decides when the plants go into the cold frame to harden off. If spring is a bit late, normal even, it will more often than not be a good idea to re-pot your plants again. This time I put them in 2 litre pots, same as before, just covering the old root ball with new compost. The way to decide whether or not to re-pot is to check the base of the pot they are in. If you can see more than one or two little roots don't delay, pot them up again. It is worth doing even if they are only likely to be in these bigger pots for a week, better than let them get even slightly pot bound. If there is the chance of even a slight frost I move them back inside for the night. The 'critical' temperature is about 3 degrees 'C' combined with a clear sky; if I see a '0' degrees forecast anywhere near on the forecast maps, then the plants get a piece of bubble wrap, bubbles down, as well. I still continue the alternate feed and water all this time. The 'trick' is to keep the plants growing slowly, even a little on the 'hard side', too much feed, or water combined with high temperatures in a greenhouse this time of year will result in lush soft growth, not what we want at all.

By the third week in May you more or less have to take the chance and plant them out. If all has gone well then your plants should be fairly hard. This combined with a sheet of bubble wrap or fleece should mean they will survive the odd chilly night.

When planting out remember what I said about planting to a stake with fruit trees, well the same applies here, except this time the stake needs to be vertical. I usually stand my plants out in their positions for a day or two before planting, dependant of course on the weather, wind isn't good either as a chill breeze can scorch the tender top leaves.

To plant, simply take out a spade full of soil where the plant is to go, knock in a stake on the side of the hole the wind usually comes from and plant your tomato plant to the stake, disturbing the roots as little as possible. One little tip - try the plant, still in its pot, to check the hole is deep enough, again aim to plant it just a little deeper, so the top of the soil in the pot is just covered. Tie the plant to the stake with soft, strong string just above the first truss using a loose figure of eight; water in, using a can or a gentle hose. Keeping the row straight is quite important as it will make things easier later. I continue with the weak feed and water alternately until the first tiny tomatoes are visible, add extra ties in the same way as before as the next truss grows. I said about knocking in the stake, ideally this stake should be about four feet long and about an inch and a half square; if you get it right you will need the strength, canes are quite inadequate.

From the day you get your plants, unless you have opted for a bush type, remove side shoots as soon as you can, they will snap out cleanly by pulling them downwards. Keep on top of this chore it will make a lot of difference to your crop.

This is going to sound daft now - if you are a smoker always wash your hands before touching your plants, especially before removing side shoots. I smoke and I never used to bother, another 'old wives tale'! Oh no it's not!! There is a horrible thing called 'T.M.V' [tobacco mosaic virus], if one of your plants gets it, the lot will have it before the week is up. You get pitted fruit, the leaves go mottled and die almost over night, and a plant laden with fruit just beginning to ripen will be dead within ten days. It happened to me, once! Never again!

This is the one down side to the variety I always grow; it is much more susceptible to T.M.V. than any other variety I know. In spite of this it is still the biggest 'no brainer' when it comes to choosing your variety, the only choice is 'Money Maker', it has been around since the Victorians, and nothing comes near it for all round performance in the garden. Another 'oldie' which does well is 'Ailsa Craig', I know it's an onion as well! There is one draw back with Ailsa Craig, get it right and the trusses get so long even the third one will reach the ground bringing your fruit in easy reach of slugs, snails, blackbirds and I've even caught a thirsty hedgehog scoffing one which was nearly ripe!

A couple of other little tips, as a general rule I take the tops out of the plants two leaves above the fourth truss. Only if my plants have gone out early and are growing exceptionally well will I allow a fifth truss; four or five, always leave two leaves above the top truss.

Although I rarely water my plants for more than a week after they have been planted out, I do use my hose pipe on them early most evenings. I squirt them as hard as I dare without breaking them, only a quick spraying over and early enough to allow them to dry off before dark. Why? Well it knocks the plants about and improves pollination meaning a lot of extra fruit.

You may find the skins are a little tougher than on many bought ones, but wait until you eat one, all the messing about is worth it.

What else do I do? Not a lot really - top dress with about an inch of sieved compost about every ten days, and remove all the shoots as soon as possible, this includes odd leaves which often appear on the trusses. The other thing I do is remove the lower leaves as the soil level rises with the top dressing. I only remove those dying or in contact with the ground; I will also remove odd leaves to allow sun and air to get at ripening fruit. To remove an old leaf cleanly, push the base of the leaf stem upwards with your thumb.

I said about keeping the row straight; things being what they are it is inevitable there will be a frost long before all the fruit has developed fully, never mind ripened. What I do is surround the row with bubble wrap, a single layer will suffice. To keep this in place I use a couple of old aviary doors covered with weld mesh, simply leaned together against the stakes this works well, and illustrates my point about using what is at hand for a particular job.

Some people will want to grow bush types or 'cherry toms' in tubs on their patio. Fair enough, as long as you have the time to look after them, and they can be fun as well as tasting good. Reading my ramblings you will have gathered I am not a fan of growing tomatoes in grow bags, of course good crops can be grown in them, but I don't care how much care and time you lavish on a couple of tomato plants in a grow bag, I would be surprised if you didn't get twice as many off one plant grown properly in the ground with a lot less effort and expense. To get good crops out of a grow bag requires very accurate watering and feeding, not easy skills to master.

So you want to grow a couple of plants on the patio in tubs - the first thing is get a good big tub, the more restricted the roots the greater the level of care required; ideally something at least two feet deep and the same across should be adequate. Half fill your container with a half and half mixture of sieved soil and sieved compost; gently firm this down. I use a large flower pot or a piece of flat board. The top half I use the contents of a grow bag, add it a couple of inches at a time; it is worth while mixing the first layer into the top of the soil/compost mix, it only needs to be the top inch or so, just to 'blend' the transition.

On the assumption you have bought a couple of plants of one of the bush varieties, they will no doubt be quite soft. If you plant them out directly then arrange some protection on cold days and on most nights! It does not have to freeze to check your plants, and a tub which is big enough to grow decent tomatoes will be too heavy to easily move inside every night. One ingenious friend of mine got round this problem by cutting down a damaged wheelie bin! He cut the damaged top off, so it was about two feet deep, a couple of hand grips in the side with the wheels, a few drainage holes, and the jobs a 'good 'un'. The other thing to watch is the watering; it is important to 'harden off' these plants without checking their growth; by keeping them 'on the dry side' for a few days you will notice the leaves turning a darker green, the last thing we want is floppy, rank growth.

Growing a 'bush' type is not a lazy option as these take just as much looking after as conventional plants. Bush types fruit on lateral shoots, these need to be stopped after the second truss, again leaving two leaves above the second truss. Stop the 'leader' or main shoot when you have four to six good side shoots, depending on how strong your plant is.

There is no point in trying to be greedy, any more than this and any fruit will not mature, never mind ripen. Make your plants concentrate on developing only those fruit which will mature before the growing season ends. I will even cut the ends off later trusses, when it becomes obvious they will never make it. No matter how hard you try you always end up with a load of green tomatoes at the end of the season, so what do you do with these? I cut the trusses off close to the stem with my secateurs, then hang them up in the greenhouse. I pick off the little ones and throw them on the compost heap; the larger green ones, which are nearly mature, are presented to the wife to make green tomato chutney. I've no idea what else she puts in it, but it tastes brilliant at Christmas with a bit of cheese or cold meat. The remainder, the most mature fruits, are left hanging on the old trusses and many will ripen like this. Any left after a couple of weeks are best used in a second batch of chutney or thrown away as they will not be good eating if left any longer.

So why don't I grow my tomatoes in my greenhouse? Well, apart from the fact I like my outdoor toms, the answer is largely because it is easier and I get much better crops. I use my greenhouse to raise many different seedlings and these require different conditions to grow well.

CHAPTER TWENTY

CROPS IN THE GREENHOUSE

If you have a greenhouse in which you can grow crops, as opposed to raising plants, then I would suggest there are other crops you could grow which would not normally grow well outside. There are three which spring to mind - cucumbers, peppers and aubergines. As I rarely grow the latter two, I can hardly offer definitive advice. It is important to get them going early, the beginning of April at the very latest, this in turn means sowing in February which will require heat. It is usually cheaper to buy a few plants from a nursery, both will respond to light, regular top dressings of sieved compost, just a light covering every ten days is enough. The principle effect of this is to keep the soil warm and moist, both hate 'cold feet' and often curl up and die, simply because the soil is too cold and wet! As with many other things in gardening it is a balance, as a 'rule of thumb' the colder your soil, the dryer it needs to be, even so the plants will still need a little water. The commonest mistake is to pour on extra water if there happens to be a couple of bright warm days early on in the season, the weather promptly returns to type for a week and.....! So gradually increase your water, don't swamp your plants.

If you like working in your greenhouse then by all means try cucumbers; these take more looking after than any other crop I know. I do grow them, not every year. Personally I don't like them, at least the long greenhouse varieties, not withstanding all the messing around. If you have time on your hands it is a satisfying crop to grow if you like a challenge. Hot and humid is the rule with these things, get it right and you can literally see the things grow, well the tendrils at least.

Before you do anything else get your wires in, starting about two feet above the ground you need horizontal wires about every foot or foot and a half at the most, all the way up to the ridge, these need to go through supporting eyes every three or four feet. It might be a good idea to provide a couple of stout supports for your greenhouse, these things are heavy. Prop up the roof and the ends as there will be a lot of tension as well as weight trying to pull the ends inwards.

Again I would buy a couple of plants; with two good plants you will be able to supply half the street if you get it right. There are so many methods recommended for growing cucumbers it would take a book on its own to describe all of them, so I will restrict myself to one which can be fun, if you have the time. Given the choice I would grow mine on an old rotting bale of wheat straw; these days it is almost impossible to get a manageable size bale, this also requires about six weeks for the bale to rot enough, so this is a non starter for me.

Bear with me - some time between Christmas and New Year I dig out a trench in the greenhouse, the outer edge about a foot from the side, two spades wide and a full spade's depth. Into this goes a generous barrow load of compost, only any really large bits are removed. This is dug into the bottom of the trench, then lightly firm it down. Now I venture out into the cold again and get a big barrow load of sifted compost; this is thoroughly mixed with the soil out of the trench. Fill your trench with this mixture so it is just level full but no more, place five or six 'seed' potatoes in a row along the centre of the trench and carefully heap the remaining soil/compost mixture in a neat ridge over them.

This is how I manage to have new potatoes before my birthday in mid May; these will produce two feeds at best. The real bonus is the 'conditioning' effect the potato plants and the compost have on the soil.

Having removed and eaten the potatoes, I then add another barrow full of the best compost I have, sieved of course. One little trick which can help give your cucumbers a flying start - having levelled your compost, get a grass box full of fresh lawn mowings and spread a layer about an inch thick over the top. Add a light sprinkling of the same magnesium limestone I recommended for your compost heap. It doesn't need a lot, a couple of three and a half inch pot fulls is enough, now dig the lot in with your spade. If you haven't got any lime than I would suggest using only a very little grass, I would still use a little as the heat it generates will help.

By this time my cucumber plants will be in two or even three litre pots. It is important to keep them growing strongly. By this time I would expect them to be near, or even at the top of a three foot cane pushed in all the way to the bottom of the pot. As usual plant them about an inch deeper than they had been in the pot, water them in and stand back!

Now the real work begins training the things.

As usual I take the lazy way and plant the cucumber plants with the cane against the wires, once I have filled in the hole, settling the soil around the root ball and watering it in, I tie the cane to the wires. For once I do not firm the plants in, the water will do that for me, to a point; the looser you can keep the soil, the better. I tend to water heaviest about a foot away from the plants, applying only enough in the area around the stems to keep the plant growing steadily; by watering away from the plant this will encourage the roots to spread out more than they would if you only water around the stems. I usually leave it about ten days before I give them the first weak feed.

It is important to keep the plants under control; turn your back on them for a week once they have settled in and begun to grow and they will have taken over! To avoid things turning into a jungle training exercise, it is a good idea to start as you mean to carry on. Having planted the cucumbers and tied in the stake, I get a length of strong string and tie one end to an anchor point on the ridge of the greenhouse level with a plant. Working down towards the plant I tie it to each wire in turn, keeping it just tight but with no real tension on it. I pass the string behind the wire, bring it out under the wire and upwards, now pass it behind the string and bring it forwards again passing in front of the wire, gently tighten it and go on down to the next wire, easy! When I reach the top wire to which the cane has been tied, I use the same twist as on the other wires then finish of with two half hitches on the diagonal around the wire and the cane, one left to right and the other right to left forming a cross and holding everything in place.

As the cucumber plant grows, I gently twist it around this strong string, the aim being to get in one complete twist between each wire. I also tie in the stem with soft string using a figure of eight at least once between each wire. I remove the growing point as soon as the plant reaches the top wire.

Apart from all this there is the watering and feeding to keep up with as well as the task of removing the tendrils unless they are serving to support a particular section of the plant; this may seem pointless but the nutrient and effort the plant expends on these things would be better diverted to producing cucumbers. In the wild these tendrils are vital in enabling the plant to climb into the light; tying it to our supports means the tendrils serve no useful purpose and are therefore wasted effort.

Depending on the variety you have chosen to grow there may be another daily chore - this is removing any male flowers. The last thing you want is for the flowers to be pollinated, if this happens you will have cucumbers fat at one end and almost pointed at the other end. These are known as 'stung' fruit and are more often than not inedibly strong or bitter.

It is not difficult to tell male from female flowers - the 'girls' will have a tiny baby cucumber between the base of the flower and the leaf axil from which it has grown; the male flowers simply have a short stem and usually appear a few days before a female flower emerges from the same leaf axil. I simply pinch out these male flowers using my thumb and forefinger, taking care not to damage any other buds growing from the same leaf joint.

Now the fun begins; not only will most leaf axils produce flowers, they will also produce lateral shoots, these will produce the majority of your cucumbers. It may sound an odd thing to do but I remove not only all flowers, male or female, as well as any laterals which try to grow within a couple of feet of the ground. Above this level tie in your lateral shoots to the wires, removing the growing points after five or six leaves have formed. Again, carefully twist the shoots around the wires and use figure of eight knots to tie them to the wire. Try to avoid more than one shoot per wire; these will of course produce side shoots of their own. Stop these at two leaves otherwise things will get totally out of control and you will have a 'Dr. Livingstone I presume' moment when you attempt to get at your crop!

The other thing to watch are the old leaves. The first to remove are those closest to the ground as they will get grotty with all the splashing from the feed and water; this usually happens around the same time as the tip reaches the top of your wires. The other source of trouble comes from any leaf pressing against the glass; the problem with these is two fold - the first cause is simple scorching from our blistering summer sun!? The leaf takes on the appearance of a piece of paper and should be removed if more than about a third of its area is affected.

The other problem with these leaves near the glass is they tend to get missed when you give them your heavy spraying over with your hose pipe after tea. There are two things which will get a hold on these 'dry' leaves - the first is powdery mildew, which amazingly has the appearance of the leaf having been dusted with a fine white powder. The other is a delightful little varmint called 'red spider mite'. I need my reading glasses to see these sneaky little pests, the first sign is usually the leaves take on a 'silky' appearance, this is the effect of their webs.

Of course there are sprays to control both of these afflictions, there is also water! It will not stop either totally but combined with removing any infected leaves it will control both. This might seem obvious, but it is a good idea to check for both before you turn on the tap and remove any infected leaves before hosing the plants down. Why? Well when the water hits the plants it will only spread both the red spider and the spores of the powdery mildew fungus, oh, and did I say you will need a towel if you spray it over first!

If you do get either of these problems, maybe I should have said 'when', you can still put the infected leaves on the compost heap. If you spot trouble and are going to remove the infected leaves, get your lawnmower out first, fill the grass box and leave it beside your compost heap, do your surgery and cover the leaves straight away with the grass. If the heat doesn't destroy the pests the liquid will. Now hose the greenhouse down. One little thing to remember - when trimming leaves, or those shoots you missed last time, use a sharp knife to get clean cuts close to the stem; it is important not to leave long, rough ended stubs, an invitation to all sorts of rot. I use a 'stanley' knife with a piece of thick 'elastoplast' on my thumb before I start, more often than not I'd need one afterwards.

And you still want to grow cucumbers!? You must like them!

CHAPTER TWENTY-ONE

OTHER 'FAMILY' MEMBERS

There is another type of cucumber which to be honest I quite like. These are the 'ridge' cucumbers, more like a giant gherkin, and are quite happy growing outside without all the fuss and palaver of staking and trimming. The variety I grow is an old one, which is getting hard to find, it is called 'King of the Ridge'. There is another good cropper called 'Burpless', no it's not! Not with me anyway. I grow these in exactly the same way as my marrows, started off in 31/2 inch pots in the greenhouse, 1 seed per pot grown in my usual mix of half and half old grow bag and sieved compost. Sown in early to mid April, all you have to do is keep them lightly watered, neither soaking them nor allowing them to dry out. Keep the slugs away, you can safely use slug killer inside, and you should have good strong plants to go outside in the second week in May.

I have put outdoor cucumbers and marrows together as they not only have the same growing requirements but both are 'dual usage' crops. The ridge cucumbers make excellent pickled gherkins if picked small - simply select one or two cucumbers to leave then pick and pickle the others when about 2 inches long. Don't be put off by the fact this variety is a bit prickley, they are one of the easiest to grow and taste great. With the marrows I use the standard 'Green

Bush' variety. These also make excellent courgettes if you pick them when they are 8 to 10 inches long, smaller if you prefer. Equally left to mature, they are one of the best marrows for 'stuffing' or cooked with a bit of butter. No, I don't know how the wife cooks them! Ask Delia or someone who does. One of my more eccentric neighbours often begs a basket of the large yellow male flowers to presumably cook and eat. I must pluck up the courage to accept her offer of a true vegetarian meal, if only to find out what she does with them. I am assured by others they taste good, so.....

Right, how to grow the things? These are really difficult! Dig out a trench, two spades wide and the full depth of the spade, sounding familiar? Keep all the soil in two neat rows, one either side of your trench. Using your fork, shake out enough compost to half fill your trench, only removing the very biggest pieces; dig this in as deep as you can. Now get some more compost, this time pass it through a one inch screen; get enough to fill what remains of your trench. Use your rake to pull the soil from one side over this compost, and mix it in with your fork; shape the mound with your rake, then pull the other ridge of soil over it to complete the ridge. This covering of soil, as opposed to a soil/compost mix, will help conserve moisture. All that remains is to plant your young marrow or cucumber plants along the crown of the ridge, two and a half to three feet apart is about right, I use my hands to make the holes, but a trowel works fine. Ensure they are planted so the soil from the pot is about an inch below the new soil level, water gently and the job is done.

As the plants grow keep an eye on the marrow plants, they are prone to a nasty mosaic virus. This usually shows up on the new leaves as yellow blotches and they take on a 'crispy' appearance. The young marrows [courgettes] will have pockmarks and pits on their skins; as soon as you see this, rip the plant up. Try not to touch the other plants, they will get it anyway eventually, but why hasten their demise. This is probably bad advice, but I chop the plants up with my spade and bury them immediately on the compost heap. Some will say this ensures next year's crop will be infected - this virus seems endemic anyway so why worry? I have grown courgettes commercially, on soil nowhere near where any marrows had ever been; the seed was certified as heat treated, virus free and expensive yet within ten days of the first cut the virus had appeared in one corner of the field. In spite of a ruthless effort to remove any plant which might have been infected, cutting knives were boiled, pickers given new gloves but within two weeks most of the crop was infected.

Why? A single female aphid blown on the wind could have come from an infected plant in a garden miles away, maybe a bumble bee after the pollen brought the virus in, who knows. The point being there are no practical measures I know of to avoid this, so we have to work round it. The way I cope is to make a second sowing about a week after I plant the first lot out. Doing this means just as the first crop start to decline, the second batch are just beginning. I can further extend my season by a further sowing in mid June. I usually grow about six plants in a batch.

One other little thing is relevant here; just for a bit of fun, why not get a pumpkin plant and grow it on the top of the compost heap which is for use in the coming autumn. Make a small spade sized hole in the top, fill it with soil and plant your pumpkin in early to mid May. It is just a bit of fun for the kiddies; its roots will also help break down some of the tougher bits in your heap, the improved texture will greatly outweigh any nutrient lost to the plant, which will end up in your heap itself. As I have said before, there is not that much nutrient in most compost any way, it is all about improving the soil 'condition'.

One thing to keep in mind - it is worth growing your marrows and ridge cucumbers next to your tomatoes. Before you clear any of these crops, mark the centre of each row with a bit of stick or cane. Clean up the patch when the last crop is finished, remove any weeds or plant remains then rake it level, flattening any ridges and filling any trenches which remain.

Firm it by doing 'the shuffle' then rake it again; if you were considering a new strawberry patch then this will be ideal; use the sticks as a guide as to where the rows should go.

Otherwise dig it over and leave it for the winter and use it for your sweet corn patch next year. You could use the site of one of the marrow or cucumber rows for your earliest row of potatoes, but NOT where your tomatoes were as they share too many pests and diseases.

CHAPTER TWENTY-TWO

SWEETCORN

This is one of my favourites; the grandkids like it too, consequently I tend to grow a bit more than most. Again I tend to buy three or four packets of 'cheapies' from a super- market or cut price shop. I have bought relatively expensive seed, 'F1's and the like and they have been very good. If you want to grow some for freezing then go for one of the F1 hybrids, as I explained earlier these are much more uniform which means you should be able to pick and freeze your crop over two weekends rather one or two cobs at a time spread over a month or so.

Sweet corn is a crop which really responds to heavy composting. If you are not using last season's marrow and tomato beds, dig in as much compost as you reasonably can in the autumn - the relatively coarse stuff just shaken out with a fork will do nicely. Come early April, remove any large or perennial weeds and cover your plot with a couple of inches of sieved compost. Dig this in carefully, there is no need to dig too deeply, about half the depth of your spade is about right. On all but the heaviest soils finish off with the 'shuffle'; this will greatly improve moisture retention. Of course if it is wet and your soil is sticky then stay off it after digging, the thin layer of sieved compost will allow you to walk on it to do the important digging without 'jamming' it all over the patio.

I usually sow mine, one to a 31/2 inch pot around the beginning of April, inevitably using cheap seeds there will be some small ones, these I tend to sow two to a pot. I use my usual mix of half and half old grow bag and sieved compost. To sow I simply make a hole in the centre of the soft compost with my index finger, just up to the first knuckle is about right. These should be right to 'harden off' in the cold frame around the end of the month which in turn, weather permitting, will allow planting out at the end of the first week in May. As with most pot grown vegetable plants, a sure sign they are ready to plant out is the appearance of roots in the drainage holes. These roots should generally be white and have a 'hairy' appearance near the tips, these root hairs are a sign of a healthy root system and just what we want.

The trick with sweet corn is to plant in blocks rather than a single row; if you have 20 plants then plant them in 4 rows with five in each row. This will greatly improve pollination so you get more full cobs rather than a 'bitty' half cob. Growing as much as I do goes a long way to solving this problem, four full rows of twenty plants in each row ensures excellent pollination. I plant mine a foot apart with a foot between each row.

As your plants grow you will notice little 'buds' forming just above the soil, these will develop into roots if you carefully top dress [mulch] with the inevitable sieved compost. I usually do this three times before the plants get too big, adding an inch or two each time. As soon as I have put on the final mulch I knock in a stout post on each corner of the bed, with another half way along each side and run a strong string around each side, with a couple of extra strings across the bed. This support will make a lot of difference should a gale come just as the plants are maturing.

I mentioned the pollination of the plants - unlike most things we grow, bees have no part to play. Sweet corn is a large annual grass which is pollinated by the wind. The pollen comes from the 'flower spike' at the top of the plant. If you look at the young cobs you will see a lot of thin filaments, these are called 'silks'. Each one of these has a single grain of corn at its base. Each one of these 'silks' need to catch at least one pollen grain to ensure its grain at the bottom grows properly. There is nothing wrong with giving nature a hand with this - when the pollen is ripe, you will see it blowing off in the breeze as a very fine dust, almost like smoke. Pick a calm, dry evening and work round your bed of sweet corn giving each stem a few light but sharp taps with a thin garden cane just below the top leaf. This will greatly enhance the number of grains on each cob.

Although corn benefits from extra water I avoid spraying them; if it should become very dry then I water the soil between the rows and if possible mulch immediately to conserve moisture.

I am often asked how do you know when the cobs are ready to pick? The 'silks' give you a clue - these will turn brown and then die, at least the bits you can see. When all the bits you can see have gone brown and start to dry off then it is a fairly safe bet the corn is ready to eat. Enjoy!!

When clearing the crop, use a fork to get the roots out; these can be tough. Knock off as much soil as you can, then cut the roots off with pruners. I stick the tops through my shredder; it's not too keen on this but it does make good compost. The roots go into the heap whole or chopped with a spade. If you haven't got a shredder then use your secateurs to cut the old plants into 6inch lengths. I cut them into my wheelbarrow if I can't be bothered to get the shredder out, then I can tip it straight onto the heap with the roots mixed in.

CHAPTER TWENTY-THREE

GREEN BEANS

We started the main part of this book with the Broad Bean. It seems fitting we finish the main text with the rest of this popular family. I have lumped all the green beans together as, apart from the supports for the climbing types, cultivation for all types is roughly the same.

On reflection there are more differences than I thought, however, runners and climbing varieties of 'French' beans have the same requirements. First and foremost the preparation of the growing site is everything in ensuring a reasonable crop and the preparation will sound familiar. Dig out a trench two spades in width and a full spade's depth, dig in a load of coarse compost into the bottom and mix some fine compost into the top later, just as for tomatoes or marrows. I usually do this in late March, well before the site is needed. This gives me ample time to sort out the supports. As is often the case, it has been suggested I have gone rather over the top when it comes to providing support for my climbing crops, it all comes back to using whatever is readily available. As runner beans are a crop which actually benefit from being grown in the same position year after year then it makes sense to provide supports which will last several seasons, unless you like work.

The supports for my row consist of a pair of dug in 10ft railway sleepers about 8ft above ground with a twenty foot scaffold pole along the top, held in place with some stout nails; there is another post, a 5"X5" half way along the pole. Overkill? Well maybe, but I never have the row blowing over or collapsing.

I always plant a double row with a foot between them and roughly a foot between plants. As I have a large bamboo plant I cut my own canes, says he showing off. Ideally these are about four feet long; simply push these in at each planting station, then cross over the tops of the canes, about two inches from the top. I tie these at the cross over then run the string up to the scaffold pole and tie it off securely. To complete the 'belt and braces' I run another string post to post, tying in each pair of canes in turn. The string I use for this is the infamous 'red string' from straw bales - tough, strong and virtually rot proof.

Surprisingly it is easy to tie all these up out of the way when it comes to preparing the soil for the next crop.

If you have a typical tiny modern garden and you only want a few plants, then you will be better off growing them on a 'tepee' of stout garden canes - these should be at least eight feet long. Push them well into the ground and tie them together securely at the top. I will admit, I do not like this way of growing beans; there is however one great advantage, these 'tepees' are much less likely to blow over when the wind catches them, usually when the crop is at its peak. It is important to allow for this if you are considering growing any of the climbing beans, a simple row of canes will either collapse or otherwise lay down, as canes in a row simply lack the strength and stability to support a mature crop on their own.

I have to admit I have no idea what variety of runner bean I grow as I have saved my own seed for as long as I can remember. I suppose they are my own selection of the basic scarlet runner, but they have probably hybridised with some of the other varieties I have grown over the years.

I sow the seeds singly in the usual three and a half inch pots in the same mix as I use for everything else. What I tend to do is sow enough for half the row at the end of the first week in April, and the remainder two weeks later. Why? Well I like to take a bit of a chance on getting some reasonably early beans, this can backfire badly if the weather plays up. If I do lose the first batch then I still have time to sow some replacements if I need to. As for when to plant them out - it is asking for trouble planting them out before the very end of April. The ideal plant should have a shoot about six to eight inches long and to have just filled the pots with roots; planting is done with a trowel and the plants are watered, rather than physically firmed in.

Although I love runner beans I cannot stand them when they get old and 'stringy', most of my friends say I pick mine too small; I think they leave theirs too long, it's all down to personal taste. As soon as the beans are about half way up the canes, I start to top dress with sieved compost. I only add about an inch each time; if it has been dry then I usually water the soil before I mulch. If there is one thing essential to growing good runners then under no circumstances allow them to get dry; if you do then you will get a very poor pollination. The bees will do their bit, but the plants will simply shed the baby pods if they are on the dry side. At the same time if you get them too wet then the root hairs will die and the leaves fall off!

This is the main reason for all the careful preparation, the deep digging acts as both drain and reservoir and serves as a sort of regulator helping the beans cope with all but the most extreme conditions. If you have got it right then you will rarely have a problem with too much water on any other than the heaviest of soils and in the wettest of summers. A little water combined with a light mulching will cure the drought problem, just don't get too carried away with the watering, it will never be a substitute for proper preparation.

A little aside, runner beans, and climbing French beans come in many varieties, the flowers can be red, purple, white, even pink; these can make a very decorative show, not to mention a tasty meal. The purple varieties tend to lack the vigour of the others so if you are going to grow a mixed row then it is as well to plant the purple leaved types in pairs so they do not get swamped by their more vigorous green leaved cousins.

When growing the dwarf or bush varieties, simply dig in plenty of compost into the area you will be planting these tasty beans; there is no need to go too mad and double dig, though you can if you wish.

I raise my plants in pots, but I always sow two beans in each pot. It is easy to work out how many to sow, these can be planted out at about eight or nine inches between each station. Unless you are growing for the freezer, then I would suggest sowing enough for a row every two to three weeks, starting at the beginning of April, making the final sowing around the end of May. Leave a generous foot between each row, keep them hoed and a mulch of compost will not do any harm; a good time to apply this mulch is when you see the first flowers

Again you have a wide choice of varieties. In addition to the standard green types with either round or flat pods, there are purple podded varieties as well as an excellent yellow podded variety which is well worth a try if you like something a bit different.

With all 'green beans' it is important to keep on top of the picking, it is a case of the more you pick, the more will grow. All of these are best eaten young.

The only significant problem with beans, runners or 'low' beans are slugs and snails. Growing them in pots means you can protect the vulnerable young plants with slug pellets with no danger to birds and hedgehogs. Once outside then there are a few 'old fashioned' tricks you can use - surround your plants with a row of soot works, if you can get the soot! If you live near the sea then collect a bit of seaweed and surround your plants with that, slugs and snails hate the salt and will not cross it. The other way is to put down slug traps, a jam jar sunk into the ground so it is level with the surface and half filled with either a sweet brown ale or stout. They fall in trying to get at the booze and end up 'pickled', what a way to go! In addition you can go round after dark on a damp night with a torch and pick off the offending creatures.

As I mentioned earlier, I tend to save my own seed. I usually leave a few of the best of the early pods on a plant at the end of the row. Inevitably you miss a few pods when you are picking your crop. If you know you definitely already have enough 'seed pods' then remove these pods which have 'gone over', these will not eat well so I simply throw them on the compost heap. There is another alternative with the round podded 'French' types, you can leave them in the same way as you would leave your 'seed'. With the right variety you can dry and shell these beans and store them. Come winter time, soak a handfull over night and add them to a stew or chilli con carne.

As far as saving the seed is concerned, pick the pods when they begin to dry on the plant, then spread them out to dry off on the greenhouse bench. These are best laid out on an old towel, or something similar. The reason for the cloth is simple; when they are totally dry the pods will crack open themselves, shedding the beans. When you see some of them have done this it is a good indication the beans are now totally 'ripe'. Shell them, and leave them spread out on a tray in the driest place you can find. It is worth noting this will be the time of year when we get heavy dew, so the greenhouse bench will no longer be the best place. The 'old boys' from the estate gardens used to use the boiler house. We have oil fired central heating so mine go on a shelf above our boiler for a week to dry off. I have used the airing cupboard, but the missus was not impressed. It only took one damp towel in there and I had to dry the beans all over again.

Failure to dry them properly will result in many of them going mouldy, not what we were hoping for! Store them in a paper bag in a dry place and all should be well.

CHAPTER TWENTY-FOUR

OMISSIONS

I know there are a multitude of possible crops I have hardly mentioned, never mind all the herbs. There are so many things you could try, to cover them all in detail would require a much larger work than this. In turn the book would also become repetitive and boring. That said it is worth giving a passing mention to a few. What beats a rhubarb crumble?

It is not difficult to grow in an odd corner, just add plenty of compost first, and resist the temptation to pick any the first year. Pick lightly the second season, ensuring you pull each stem off cleanly; leaving a stub is a sure way to allow in crown rot which will kill your plant. Remove any flowering stems which appear as these will sap the strength of your plant. I wouldn't try 'forcing' any for the first couple of years, after that then by all means turn an old bucket upside down over your crowns. Growing in the dark like this will produce bright tasty stems, generally less tart than exposed stems. Don't be greedy; once you have had a couple of feeds move the bucket over another root; leave enough leaves on the 'forced' root for the plant to regain its strength. Top dress with sieved compost at regular intervals when the plants are growing, keeping it off the crowns.

Remember, rhubarb leaves are poisonous. I always leave the top inch of the stem attached to the leaves when I trim them. I have seen it emphasized in some books not to put these leaves or flower stems on the compost heaps. I do, and I can't say I have ever noticed a problem. I'll bet they are a lot less toxic than some inks on the shredded paper some advocate composting, never mind the bleaches used to make the paper white.

Another crop I only mentioned in passing was Chinese leaves; new types appear almost annually and would need a book on their own. I have grown a few from time to time and quite like the ones I have tried. The basic Chinese cabbage can be used as either cabbage or lettuce and are good either way as a change from the normal fare. They do have their problems however. I have never grown anything which attracts such a wide variety of pests. If ever there was a crop designed to be grown under one of these 'insect proof', pest nets then this is it. I have to say this way makes sense if, like me, you avoid chemicals as far as possible.

Remember we are talking about the basic Chinese cabbage here, although the same applies to many of the more exotic types. Sow a pinch of seed in a pot every couple of weeks from mid March until the end of June. Pot the seedlings up, as with lettuce. If your bench is 'slatted' then remember to stand your pots on the anti-invader membrane as well as covering the plants with it.

The same applies in the frame hardening them off and make sure your 'tent' is sealed over the growing plants. The list of winged things which will eat these is long and varied; a well sealed 'tent' will stop pretty well all of them. The cabbage root fly can't get at them to lay their eggs so their 'maggots' can't chew up the roots; the various white butterflies will get positively frustrated, they know the favourite food for their caterpillars is under there somewhere!

It keeps out the cabbage moth as well so their hungry burrowing slug-like offspring can never enjoy turning the tasty hearts of your crop to revolting wet green pellets of caterpillar pooh. Best of all, the winged forms of the various aphids can't get through the fine mesh to suck the sap from your crop and cover your plants with rot attracting honey dew. I have identified seven different species of aphid on a single plant! Wood pigeons like Chinese cabbage; they will walk round one of these tents for hours in a state of confusion, 'if only I could find a way in?' Their smaller relatives, the collared doves are just as dense, but get bored quicker and go in search of an easier meal elsewhere.

If anyone comes up with an easier way of growing these tasty crops, let me know!

Another easy to grow crop is celery, whether you grow the green 'self blanching' type or the winter blanching type depends on what you want it for; as an additive to stew, in which case grow the 'fen' type which you have to earth up to blanch or the summer/autumn cropping self blanching varieties to go with your salads is a matter of personal choice.

Without doubt the self blanching types are much easier to grow. This is another crop best grown in a block rather than the usual row, much as with your sweetcorn, but for a different reason. Almost any reasonable soil will give good crops. As always, dig in a good dose of compost to your plot, then make a crude frame of wooden boards. It need not be an elaborate construction; knock in a short piece of two by two in each corner, leaving about a foot sticking up. Nail any old boards to these to give you 'walls' about a foot high. You will find it easier to cut these to length before nailing them to the posts. When knocking in the nails try putting a heavy hammer behind where you are knocking in the nail, it will be much easier and will loosen the post less. One other little tip - I avoid using treated wood as this can taint the celery; even wood treated some time ago and which no longer smells can still make the celery taste funny.

I always raise my plants in the greenhouse, sowing the seed in either a 5 inch 'half pot' or a small seed tray. If you have them, a silver foil tray such as the type you get with your 'take away' will do, just remember to make a few drainage holes.

Pot up the same as anything else, one seedling to a 31/2 inch pot or drinks cup; plant out as soon as there is a nice root ball in the pot. This 'self blanching' type can be planted out as close as six inches apart; I prefer eight inches between plants but it doesn't really matter. Water your plants in well, then cover your 'frame' with a piece of polythene, as long as it lets through enough light it need not be anything fancy; hold it tightly in place with strips of lath tacked down onto the edges of your boards.

There are a couple of reasons I do this - one, it enables me to use slug pellets safely and it draws the plants upwards; as soon as the plants reach the polythene remove it. All you have to do now is water and weed your crop, to a point the more you water this crop, the better it will be. Water the plants carefully, try to avoid splashing the soil about, so do it gently between the rows in your frame. It is not a bad idea to spray them over now and then, not to give them extra water but to let the white fly know they are not welcome. These messy little critters hate water, it not only knocks the adults about disturbing them, it drowns their eggs and babies further reducing the problem.

That just about covers the self blanching types. As for the winter variety, the plants are raised just the same way, it is the growing method which differs.

Prepare the ground in the same way as you would for tomatoes -

the trench, compost dug in etc. Plant your celery about ten to twelve inches apart in the shallow trench left after you have dug in your compost; as with the self blanching types this crop needs plenty of water. Gradually earth up your crop, using the top soil left either side of your trench. Use the same technique as with the 'show off' leeks, in other words hold the leaves together with one hand to avoid too much soil getting into the plant itself. Some soil will of course get between the leaves; don't worry too much as each 'stick' of celery will need a good scrub anyway. By the time the festive season arrives your row should have a ridge about a foot high with just a tuft of green leaves sticking out of the top. Dig out the plants as you need them; don't forget to make certain the next plant is not exposed to the air as this will quickly 'unblanch' the exposed side and spoil the crop.

As well as being great with a chunk of cheese, chopped up sticks taste great in a stew in much the same way as celeriac.

There are all sorts of 'dodges' advised for keeping the soil out of the plants - everything from wrapping them in newspaper to growing in a drain pipe. All work to a point, but the paper rots and attracts even more slugs as does the pipe. I'm not saying don't try these ideas, it is just I have found they create more problems than they cure; it is quite possible they might work for you.

This chapter could get longer than the rest of the book, but this would defeat the object so if you want to grow spinach or whatever, you are on your own.

CHAPTER TWENTY-FIVE

A SUGGESTED STARTER PLOT

So we are looking at a typical small plot on a new estate - what do you grow? All I can suggest is what I would grow on a lightish soil.

A packet of autumn sown broad beans, I will reiterate, get these from a reputable seed firm.

A few strawberries are always worth while, again, get the best plants, but start with Cambridge favourite until you get the hang of growing them, then by all means try some of the newer ones.

A bag of cheapie onion sets.

A row of early potatoes is always worthwhile.

A steady supply of lettuce alternating between the different types.

If you like the various Chinese and salad leaves then get a protective anti-bug mesh tent and sow a pinch of one or the other each week to keep a steady, varied supply going.

A row of runner beans, probably better grown on a 'tepee' of canes rather than a row, or a row of low beans.

Four or five standard tomato plants, stick to Money Maker to start with, maybe a couple of 'cherry toms' if you have kiddies.

A row of cauliflower plants, bought from the local market will be a good starter to learn on.

A couple of rows of carrots and the same of beetroot, just to get the hang of things.

If you have the space it is always worth a row of sprouting broccoli, purple or otherwise depending on your tastes.

Everyone will have different tastes but the above should cover most tastes and also help learn the different techniques to grow most crops. Good luck.

CHAPTER TWENTY-SIX

LAZY WAYS and ODDS AND ENDS

As I have said several times already, I am really a lazy 'so and so'. If I can find an easier way of achieving the same result then why not!!? We started with the premise of a bramble ridden jungle and ended with a garden full of fruit and veg hopefully achieved without a visit to 'Casualty'. It was a lot of work, some of it painstaking, all that messing about picking out all those roots, digging in the compost, some of it two spades deep.

I suppose the 'modern way' would be to hack it down, spray it once, burn most of the rubbish then rotavate it. The rotavating would be done one spring morning, probably a Saturday; the following day the plot would have been fully planted up - neat rows of cell grown plants, all the seeds sown, job done. Good luck, you'll need it! Oh dear, you forgot the fertilizer, never mind spread it over everything, it will be alright.

"I'm glad we got everything planted before we brought the kids away for Easter love." I can hear it now as you walk back to your holiday cottage in Fowey, Falmouth or where ever. The weather hasn't been great, a bit damp but not too cold.

"Did you see the weather forecast, it has been a beautiful sunny weekend back home, I'll bet things are growing in the garden."

I'll bet they are! but a lot of it won't be edible, unless you are a bug!.

Those clear sunny days produced a radiation frost on one night; this finished off soft plants whose leaves were already scorched by the drying breeze and the carelessly spread fertilizer. The few seeds which were showing signs of germinating when you left are now either dead or struggling. The top soil, turned to powder by the machine, has dried out; the only things which have thrived are the weeds, but then they are native plants. Natural selection over centuries has favoured those able to cope with the quirks of our climate. Getting home to something like this does rather spoil the afterglow of a holiday, and it was the neighbour's fault the tomatoes in the grow bag on the patio are dead, he didn't water them. "You did ask him?" Not that it would have mattered, the frost got them anyway.

So why would the 'old' approach have been better?

For a start the gardeners who used to work in the grounds of the big estate houses were expected to produce whatever 'Cook' asked for, and what 'Cook' asked for she got! These old boys had this knowledge passed on to them from generations of gardeners; the one thing they had was time! Plants are living things; try to rush them and things will not turn out as they should. It is the same with the methods we use today. Gardening is all about patience and timing; get the timing right and it is not difficult to get good results. They knew it was important to get it right first time; like I keep saying, I'm basically lazy, getting it right first time means I only have to do the job once. So when I clear a new patch I do it thoroughly, this means not only getting the rubbish out but compost in, where it is needed. With their roots into the well buried compost, I don't have to worry if I'm away during a dry spell, my crops will be fine.

This of course comes back to digging properly and brings this book full circle.

As I am lucky enough to have light, open soil I can indulge my lazy streak, in as much as I can grow up to three crops in between digging a particular patch. Following my main crop potatoes, I can plant my over wintering peas and broad beans - the soil is loose and clean after lifting the spuds; as it will not be needed for a bit, firm it down with the 'shuffle' and then add a thin layer, about an inch, of sieved compost. When the time comes to plant your broad beans or peas, clear off any weeds, then use either your hoe in a sharp chopping motion or a three tined cultivator to mix in the compost, but only on the ground you need. By all means clear any weeds off the remainder of the plot but leave it otherwise undisturbed until you need it in the spring, then cultivate it and plant your spring peas and any more beans. When these legumes have finished, tidy up the plot and you can plant your cabbages and their cousins without any further digging. Three crops since I last dug it! Suits me and my plants!! However, I would not recommend this technique until you have your soil in good condition, and of course it only works on light, open soils.

Having a very large garden means I can afford to leave a patch 'resting' after the potatoes, in a small garden it makes more sense to follow the spuds with spring cropping 'greens'. It has to be more intensive in a small garden to get the maximum crops. Personally I would still advise following the spuds, legume then brassica sequence, at least until you really have got 'the hang' of this gardening lark. The more intensively you crop your soil, the more you need to feed it and your plants. I don't care how much money you spend on feeds and fertilizers, if your soil is not in good 'condition' much of your money and effort will be wasted. There is NO substitute for a well conditioned soil; once you have achieved this then by all means step up the intensity of your cropping, maintain the compost applications and by all means use a minimal amount of feed or fertilizer. Your soil will then be able to hold this until your crops need it. Using fertilizers on poor conditioned soil will result in most of it washing away, either when it rains or you water your struggling crops. If your soil is really gutless then you will have to feed your crops. The best way is to use a folia feed - be sure to do this in the evening, preferably a cloudy one; the longer it takes to dry the more the plant absorbs. Use it weak and often - never, ever in bright sun. The modern feeds might not scorch the leaves but if it dries quickly then it will not be taken up by the hungry plants.

These days almost everyone has a patio or slab paths; weeds coming up between the slabs are a right pain. You can of course use a commercial weedkiller, there are several available in little squirty things. Fine, but this is about saving money. The easy way is to boil the kettle, then as quickly as you can carefully pour the boiling water along the cracks. Do this as soon as you see the weeds. It works a treat - it will even kill any seeds it touches, the ants don't like it either.

I was saying earlier about getting the little ones involved - the first memory I have of growing things was of growing cress in a saucer on a piece of blotting paper. Why not try it, if you like salads with cress?

As all this grow your own stuff was the wife's idea then why not get your own back. Present her with a packet of mung beans to grow in the airing cupboard. There are all sorts of bits and pieces you can try growing like this. As you get better with the easy stuff you can move on to things like mushrooms, some of them quite exotic and tasty.

Once you have things set up and running, make it a family thing.

It can be fun as well as hard work and by following the tips in this book you can reduce not only the bills but the hard work, leaving more time for the fun bit.

I suppose I had better say a little about cuttings. If herbs are your thing then many can be grown from seed but sooner or later you will come across a plant in a friend's garden that you or the wife want.

This will not work for everything but most plants can be propagated this way - what you want is a nice young shoot three inches or so long, depending what it is. Carefully remove the lower leaves, then using something very sharp, I use an old razor blade, cut cleanly just below where you pulled off a leaf. It is important to remove the leaves first as if you cut first then on many varieties you will find the bottom bud, just above your cut, will come away with the leaf, not good!. All that is left to do is to pop it into a pot filled with a mixture of sharp sand and peat, the compost from an old grow bag will do for the peat bit; water it and put the whole thing into a polythene sandwich bag. It is a good idea to put at least three little bits of cane or stick in to keep the polythene off the leaves. Don't put it in direct sunlight, most things root in a couple of weeks or so.

The rooting powders often promoted will in many cases improve your success, not so much from the rooting hormone in them which might mean the cuttings root faster, the real benefit is from the fungicide in them which will prevent some of the cuttings rotting off. It's up to you, personally I don't bother.

Gardening will also give you a chance to get to know your neighbours, work together, like a loose little co-op, share packets of seeds or plants to cut costs even more. If you have a local Mrs. Bucket [Bouquet], and it is beneath her to allow her hubby to dig up their lawn to grow veg, then he may be willing to donate his lawn mowings and hedge clippings to your compost heap. He will save on the cost of a garden waste wheelie bin or trips to the dump and you gain valuable compost.

Keep these groups small and simple. If you get too many interested, then have two groups, just order your seeds together, as bulk purchase is always cheaper. Every little group will be different - make friends, cut your bills and enjoy not only growing your own but eating the results of your efforts. Get the basics right and it is not difficult.... enjoy.

Green manure

I have mentioned green manure crops as a way of improving things before you get your compost heaps into full production. Green manure is a valuable option with a couple of provisos, the first of which is you must be able to dig reasonably well. This really matters - if you take great lumps you won't bury the crop properly and your attempts to level the ensuing uneven surface will only uncover yet more, much of which is likely to regrow.

The other thing to consider is - which crop to grow on your soil. Any reputable seed firm will offer advice on this, 'recommended for heavy soils' or best cut with a lawn mower and allowed to grow again before digging in, all good advice.

One crop I like for heavy soils and I rarely see for sale is Luceren. It is a bit longer term thing than most but the advantages are great; it is a legume, so adds nitrogen. The real benefit is it is tough with a substantial root system; given the choice I would cut it once with the mower when it is about eight to ten inches high, with the mower set as high as it will go. This of course is a rotary mower, not a drum type. You can add this to the compost heap or leave it lying. If it has grown well then it is best added to the compost heap as a dense layer of chopped up cuttings will inhibit the re-growth. When it is dug in, it really is important to take small spits as the roots form a dense wirey matt and can cause problems if left in large lumps but on a nasty heavy soil will really improve things.

For a quicker crop to achieve a similar result, though not as long lasting, then try field beans - a smaller version of broad beans. Again this crop will benefit from cutting once and allowing re-growth. If your digging is not up to scratch then go for mustard or one of the smaller, quicker green manure crops on offer and dig them in whole and early when only a few inches high.

When you sow these crops, always leave a gap for your trench to start with when you come to dig it in; there is no point in sowing right up to this edge, as you will turn some of the crop into this trench when you dig. Anything sown there will only get in the way when opening your trench.

As a really cheap skate alternative you can always allow the weeds to grow a little, some are actually quite good for this, but you do need to have the right weeds and remove any of the perennial weeds before digging the remainder in. Again they must be totally buried or many will re-grow among your crops.

This is not a book of magic, it is merely a collection of little tips and hints I have picked up over the years which have helped me to grow decent crops without spending a fortune. There is no magic formula for growing good veg, it is mainly common sense and knowing a little about what the different crops like, or don't like, such as fresh manure for carrots. It is these little things which make the difference.

Much of it is about conserving moisture and getting the soil into a condition which holds that moisture without becoming water logged. This is what getting plenty of compost deep down is all about for those crops which need adequate water; spraying over with a hose pipe is actually usually counter productive in the long run. It encourages plants to grow a lot of shallow surface roots making them even more vulnerable to drought when you go on holiday or a hose pipe ban is enforced. The other thing it does is to pan the surface down; any rain which may fall then can't easily soak in, it stays at the surface - out comes the sun, or a breeze springs up and evaporates all the rain which fell.

One thing it is worth doing is to hoe, at least once a week, only about half an inch deep, at most an inch, even if there are no weeds. The object is to form what is called a dust mulch. This is simply a thin layer of fine soil which will often totally dry out, the soil beneath it however will retain its moisture - better still any rain which falls will easily soak through into the soil below where the plants can get it.

All that remains is for me to wish you good luck in your venture, don't get too disheartened with the odd failure, it happens to us all at some time or other.

All the best Paul Rix.

Lightning Source UK Ltd.
Milton Keynes UK
171603UK00001B/79/P